PRAISE FOR GO IN PEACE FOR TEENS

I believe *Go in Peace for Teens* will be the Father's balm to hurting hearts, the Spirit's ointment to aching souls, and the Son's salve to life's trials. The Lord is using Cherie and this very practical book to help apply this salve to our teens and their hurts today.

—Brian Bell
Senior Pastor
Calvary Chapel Murrieta

Go in Peace for Teens is an awesome biblically-based workbook for guiding teens into the victory that is found only in Jesus Christ. Through wonderful word pictures and the deep abiding truth of God's Word, Cherie provides a safe path for exploring and resolving the root causes of hurt, pain and anger. I have used Cherie's first book, *Go in Peace,* to minister to my incarcerated girls at Juvenile Hall for many years, and I am blessed to have this new tool specifically tailored to the needs of young people.

—Sheri Snyder
Para-Chaplain
Orange County Juvenile Hall, CA

Go in Peace for Teens is an insightful, timeless, and biblically-principled roadmap to the life of freedom and victory that only Jesus can bring. It's an easy read, with practical step-by-step biblical solutions to the problems all teens suffer from today. Every teen needs to read this book—it will truly be life changing.

—Monty W. Sharp
Director, Student Venture
Riverside County, CA

Go in Peace for Teens is a tremendous resource to help youth who are stuck in a negative cycle break free to hope and healing. I am glad our organization can offer this book to our country's most angry, scared, and hurting teens. I highly recommend it for every "at-risk" kid— which includes yours and mine.

—Victor Marx
Author and Speaker
President, All Things Possible Ministries

I finished the *Go in Peace for Teens* lessons, and I thought they were great! The book covered a lot of issues I have. I loved it! I wrote down all of the verses at the end of each lesson and kept them in my Bible! Thank you so much for sending it to me!

—Scarlett, Age 18
Incarcerated

Go in Peace for Teens has moved me in countless ways. I found truth and the representation of God's love penned within its pages. From the first chapter, my heart felt God pulling me ever closer to Him. *Go in Peace for Teens* has helped me to realize that Satan has had a foothold on my life and how my sin, which took its form in hurt, anger, and distrust, was putting an empty void between me and my heavenly Father. God used *Go in Peace for Teens* to help me find myself and Him and, for the first time, grasp true hope and the necessary tools needed for lasting change. *Go in Peace for Teens* helped me cast aside my hurt and, regardless of the pain, find healing and purpose in Christ.

—Dierdre, Age 16

CHERIE
FRESONKE

GO IN
PEACE
FOR TEENS

WINEPRESS **WP** PUBLISHING

All clip art is from © 2009 Jupiterimages Corporation or © 1997 T/ Maker Company, Broderbaud Software, Inc. [Except for Tabernacle diagram which was created by Cherie Fresonke and arrows which were created by Matthew Laster. Used by permission.]

WinePress Publishing (PO Box 428, Enumclaw, WA 98022) functions only as book publisher. As such, the ultimate design, content, editorial accuracy, and views expressed or implied in this work are those of the author.

ISBN 13: 978-1-57921-980-2
ISBN 10: 1-57921-980-2
Library of Congress Catalog Card Number: 2008932084

Contents

ACKNOWLEDGMENTS

My full gratitude and acknowledgment—first and foremost—goes to my Lord and Savior. He is the author and finisher of our faith. I thank Him for all He has done in and through my life. I thank Him for what He has taught me, which I can now share with you. And I thank Him for how He guided me in writing this book. Each morning as I sat down to write, I had such comfort in knowing that, because He is the author and finisher of my life, He already knew exactly what words were to be on each page. He saw the book finished, even though all I saw was a blinking cursor on a blank screen. There is no way I could have completed even one page of this book without Him.

I also thank God for the teens He has brought my way, who were willing to share their deep heart hurts with me, so that I could listen to the Lord as He guided me to share His love and truth with them. May each one of you *go in peace* all the days of your life.

I also want to thank God for everyone He put into my life to help me complete this book: to those who have gone before me in serving the Lord, and who have faithfully shared what He taught them through the books and sermons I gleaned from. To Calvary Chapel Murrieta, who allowed some of my working hours to be spent on writing this book, which helped me tremendously to make time in my busy schedule to write: thank you! To my wonderful sister, who challenges me to be specific in every detail of my writing. She also helped field-test the book with teens in Juvenile Hall. To Kathie, who would listen and brainstorm ideas with me. She, too, helped field-test the book with teens. To my editor, who helped me with all those confusing commas. I don't know if I will ever get them all right. To my daughters, who shared their stories in this book and also helped around the house so that I could write. To my husband, my best friend, who on his days off willingly slept late so that I could write in the early morning in peace and quiet. I'll always remember our wonderful early morning joke: "Go to sleep!"

Finally, I want to thank each person, beforehand, who will someday share this book with a hurting teen. Rewards await you in heaven for your compassion.

"Looking unto Jesus, the author and finisher of our faith."

—Hebrews 12:2a NKJV

HOW TO USE
THIS BOOK

This book can be used for individual study, or it can be used as a Bible study in one-on-one discipleship by pastors, counselors, and other youth leaders who want to minister to hurting teenagers. It is also a great book for parents to use to better understand their teenagers.

Individual Study

If you are reading through this book on your own, please take the time to read and complete all of the exercises before moving on to the next chapter. The book was not written to be read through quickly—it has been written for you to read slowly and ponder what you have read. *Ponder* means "to consider something deeply and thoroughly." [1] With this in mind, read one chapter one day, taking the time to consider and think about what you learned, and then complete the "Digging Deeper" section the next day, taking the time to ponder the verses listed there. The verses hold key information about who you are in Christ! After you have done this, continue to ponder what you learned in the chapter for a day or so. When you have thought about the material in that chapter, considered it deeply, and applied it to your life, then move on to the next chapter. If you truly take to heart what is taught within this book, your life will be impacted in an amazing way. You will be set free from whatever you are struggling with. Best yet, you will *go in peace!*

One-on-One Bible Study

If you are taking a teen through the book as part of a Bible study, I recommend that you go through one chapter of the book per week. Read the chapter out loud as the teen reads along in his or her own book, and then have him or her answer the questions in the chapter out loud. This will help you get to know the teen on a more personal level. The only exception to this is during the first session; complete both the introduction and chapter one together. The introduction includes a section for the teen to list his (or her) goals for working through the book, so make sure to cover this material before you begin working through the first chapter.

At the end of each chapter is a section titled "Digging Deeper." This section is for the teen to complete on his (or her) own, before meeting for the next session. Each chapter usually takes about 30 minutes to cover, but you might want to schedule an hour for the appointment so that you have plenty of time to talk about what is going on in the teen's life that week. It is amazing how God can use the material in the chapters to meet the teen right where he (or she) is each week. The teen can begin to see that God really does care. Also, the book is written so that if the teen cannot complete the book with you, he (or she) can still complete it on his (or her) own.

Parents

If you see your teen struggling with guilt, shame, fear, anxiety, depression, rage, relationship difficulties, or self-destructive behaviors such as anorexia, bulimia, cutting, or harming themselves, drugs, alcohol, or suicidal thoughts, then know that more than likely, he or she is reacting to hurt deep within the heart that has not been dealt with in the manner God intended. This hurt can be a huge issue, such as rape or abuse, or the hurt can be a smaller issue, such as gossip or rejection. No matter what the issue, it can be destructive to your teenager if it is not handled appropriately. So how do you, as a parent, respond? Through prayer! Ask God for His wisdom in how to work with your teen. God created each one of us individually, so there is not one pat answer as to how parents should respond to their hurting teen. And while you are praying, take the time to read through this book, asking God to give you insight into your teenager. God is faithful, and if you are willing to listen, He will guide you.

May God do a mighty work! *Go in peace!*

> "And we desire that each one of you show the same diligence so as to realize the full assurance of hope until the end."
>
> —Hebrews 6:11 NASB

INTRODUCTION

When I was a kid, I had my share of deep heart hurts. Believe me, we live in a sinful world, and by a young age I had seen my share of sin. Much of the muck of our sinful world splashed on me. Alcoholism, abuse, and divorce were just a few of the hurtful things I had to deal with. Unfortunately, I was never taught as a child what to do with these feelings of pain, and so I, like most kids my age, stuffed it deep within my heart. As a result, these deep heart hurts became infected and began to poison my whole life.

By the time I was a teen, I was acting out on the infection within my heart. Without even realizing it, I got caught up in a vicious downward spiral of sin, sin, and more sin. This infection and downward spiral caused me to make some very foolish choices that added to my deep heart hurt—foolish choices about wrong relationships, alcohol, drugs, sexual immorality, and abortion. As a result, I struggled with fear, depression, anxiety, and rage, to name just a few of the things associated with deep heart hurts. There seemed to be no way out. I was caught in the miry pit. Or so I thought.

When I was ready to admit that my life was out of control, I cried out to God for help and He met me there. He began to heal my broken heart and taught me how to give my deep heart hurts to Him once and for all. I learned that He never intended for me to carry the hurt by myself. What He taught me set me free. It enabled me to *go in peace!* Fear was replaced with strength, depression with joy, anxiety with faith, and rage with rest. Best yet, I experienced peace with God deep within my heart. That's what it means to *go in peace!*

All of us live in a sinful world. Because of this, we will encounter hurts. Often, these hurts result from our own foolish actions and choices—like the downward spiral of sin, sin, and more sin that I was caught up in as a teen. Or they may be the result of another person's sin against us—like the abuse I experienced as a young child. In either case, what we do with this hurt greatly affects us. It can cause us to dwell in a miry pit of despair filled with fear, depression, anxiety, and rage, to name just a few.

If you have been hurt like I was, this book is for you. As the prophet Isaiah once wrote:

> Why should you be beaten anymore? Why do you persist in rebellion? Your whole head is injured, your whole heart afflicted. From the sole of your foot to the top of your head there is no soundness—only wounds and welts and open sores, not cleansed or bandaged or soothed with oil.
>
> —Isaiah 1:5–6

God loves you deeply. He never intended for you to stuff the hurt deep within your heart. He always intended for you to give it to Him so that He can cleanse it, soothe it, and heal it completely. In this book, you will learn to recognize your deep heart hurts and see if they have become infected. You will learn how to give your hurts to God in the way He intended, so that you too can *go in peace!*

Before we begin, I want you to make a list of goals. Now, these are not goals like what you want to do after you graduate from college, but spiritual goals. I want you to list what you want God to do in your life about your deep heart hurts. Let me give you some examples I hear over and over again when I work with teenagers: *I want to be set free from the hurt. I want to be set free from the anger. I want to be set free from the depression or anxiety. I want the strength to stop the alcohol or drugs. I don't want my deep heart hurts to affect my family and loved ones. I want to forgive the person who hurt me. I want to know that God forgives me for the wrong I have done. I want to draw closer to God. I want my life to have meaning. I want to be used by God and help other people. I want to go in peace.*

You can write down your list of goals following the introduction. As you write, think about the following:

- What do you want God to do in your life through this book?

- Do you have a deep heart hurt that needs healing?

- Have you done something that you need to know God forgives you for?

- Do you want to be set free from hurt, fear, depression, anxiety, rage, alcohol, drugs, suicidal thoughts, or other things associated with your deep heart hurt?

- Do you desire to know why God gave you life?

- Do you want to be used by God to help others?

Write down whatever your goals are. When you finish reading the book, we will take a look at these goals once again. It is remarkable how God will help you meet these goals. It is awesome! This is a practical way for you to see how God is working in your life.

In the back of the book, you will find three appendices called "Cruddy Consequences," "Answers to Questions," and "Profile of an Abuser." You will learn about the section titled "Cruddy Consequences" in chapter 3. The section titled "Answers to Questions" has all the answers for the questions in the book. Try to answer the questions that you find in the chapters on your own, but if you are stuck or want reassurance, you can check your answer in the back. Also included is a section called "Profile of an Abuser." It is important to know how an abuser acts when you first enter the dating or courting scene so that you can know the warning signs to watch for. If you see any warning signs, get out of that relationship before it is too late!

I pray that God will do a mighty work in your life concerning your deep heart hurts. If you will open your heart to the truth that you will learn within these pages, you will truly find "the peace of God, which surpasses all understanding" (Philippians 4:7, NKJV). I also pray that you will find in these pages a love for you that is so deep, it's almost unimaginable. God desires for you to discover this love so you can *go in peace!*

GOALS

What do you want God to do in your life through reading this book? Make a list of your spiritual goals below.

_____

_____

_____

_____

_____

_____

_____

_____

_____

_____

_____

_____

_____

_____

_____

_____

_____

_____

_____

_____

_____

_____

YOU ARE LOVED

Over the years I have worked with many teenagers, both in America and in Eastern Europe. One of the things I have discovered in my travels is a desire among teens to get married and have a family. I find this true for everyone I meet—both guys and girls. I believe this desire comes from a deep longing within each of our hearts to simply be loved—to be loved for who we are.

When I was young, I had a keychain that read, "To know me is to love me." Isn't that how we all feel deep inside? If only someone would take the time to get to know me, then they would really love me.

So let's begin with this topic of love. You need to know that Someone loves you deeply. No matter what you feel, what you have been through, or what you have done—both good and bad—you are loved deeply. You see, although the world teaches that you are a mere mistake—that you came to be as a result of evolution—the truth is that you were created in

1

God's own image. You were knit together in your mother's womb and are a work of art. You are not a mistake! No matter what others may have told you or what you may feel, the truth is that you were created by a Creator with a specific purpose in mind. Knowing and understanding this truth can help bring you to a place of completely believing that you are deeply loved.

As we go through each chapter, I will share many truths with you. These truths are not simply what I believe, but are actual truths from God Himself found in the Bible. What God has to say is much more important than anything I have to say, so we will be looking at a lot of verses from the Bible. If any of these verses speak to your heart, make sure you put a little * or √ next to it. After you complete the chapter, you can then look up the verses in your Bible and highlight them so that you can easily find them again.

Jeremiah 31:3 says:

> The Lord appeared to us in the past, saying: "I have loved you with an everlasting love; I have drawn you [wooed you] with loving kindness."

According to Jeremiah 31:3, what has God drawn you with?

_____

_____

_____

According to this verse, how has He loved you?

_____

_____

_____

Based on what you read in this verse, are you loved by God? Tell the truth. Don't write down what you feel, but what the truth of God's Word says.

_____

_____

_____

Write the truth that you are loved.

I am _____

Psalm 31:21 is another wonderful verse about the love of God:

> Praise be to the LORD, for he showed his wonderful love to me.

Many times, I think we don't believe the truth of God's Word when it says that we are loved because of the deep hurt that is within our hearts. It is as if this deep hurt causes such a scarring on the outside of our hearts that we don't allow the truth of God's love to penetrate to the inside of our hearts. It is as if our hearts are covered by a big, thick, disgusting scab and scar tissue. Worse yet, our hearts are not only covered by scabs and scar tissue, but are also infected deep within, which can poison our whole lives.

Take a look at a particular verse that is repeated twice in the Bible. Proverbs 18:8 and 26:22 describe an interesting truth:

> The words of a gossip are like choice morsels; they go down to a man's inmost parts.

I call this verse the "cow verse." Yes, that's right, "cow."

You see, when someone says or does something to hurt us deeply, we can't stop thinking about it. We keep replaying the words or hurtful act over and over again in our heads. Then, when we can't stand it any longer, we shove the hurt deep within our hearts, deep within our inmost beings. It is as if we had swallowed it. Once swallowed, we think it is gone. We think that we are over the hurt, and so we try to move on with our lives.

But then, when we least expect it, something reminds us of that hurt and it all comes back again—all the bad memories and all the hurt and pain. Then we start thinking about what we experienced all over again. As we do this, we are like cows chewing on our cud.

The word *cud* means "food brought up into the mouth by some animals [such as cows] from the rumen [a part of their stomach] to be chewed again."[1] In other words, cud is *gross*. It is grass or feed that a cow has chewed up, swallowed, burped up, re-chewed, re-swallowed, re-burped up and then chewed on some more. The people who count these things tell us that dairy cows spend an average of 8 hours a day chewing their cud—for a total of almost 30,000 chews each day.[2]

We are like cows chewing the cud!

Do you now understand how we are like cows? That is what we do when we continue to stuff or swallow the hurt and pain deep within our hearts, deep within our inmost beings. When we don't give the hurt and pain to God in the manner He intended, we are stuffing it deep inside. Then when we least expect it, when something reminds us of the past hurt, we burp it up and chew on it some more. When this happens, the verse in Proverbs becomes true in our lives: "The words of a gossip are like choice morsels; they go down to a man's inmost parts" (Proverbs 18:8; 26:22).

Many times, the cud of hurt and pain that we choose to chew on is a result of sin. This sin can be self-inflicted or inflicted by another. Self-inflicted sins occur as a result of our own foolish actions and choices—something that we have control over. Sins inflicted by another are those sins that happen as a result of others doing something to hurt us—something we have no control over. Let me give you some examples of these two categories of sin.

Self-Inflicted Sin	Sin Inflicted by Another
Results from our own foolish choices, including:	*Results from others doing something to hurt us, including:*
• Bad Decisions	• Gossip
• Wrong Choices	• Rejection
• Lies	• Mean Pranks
• Drugs and/or Alcohol	• Abuse (verbal, physical, sexual)
• Sexual Immorality	• Rape
• Abortion	
The List Is Endless	The List Is Endless

As I mentioned in the introduction, my life unfortunately has examples of both categories of sin. My self-inflicted sins included such foolish choices as wrong relationships, alcohol, and drugs, sexual immorality, pregnancy outside of marriage, and abortion. I had control over each of these sins—they were a result of my own foolish actions and choices. Sins inflicted by another on me, which caused me deep heart hurt from a very young age, included alcoholism, abuse, and the divorce of my parents. These were sins I had no control over—they were the sins of another which caused me hurt and pain.

What are some of the self-inflicted sins which have caused you pain?

_____

_____

_____

What are some of the sins inflicted by another which have caused you hurt?

_____

_____

_____

Whatever the sin—whether self-inflicted or inflicted by another—what we do with the hurt as a result of the sin can greatly affect us and cause us to jump into what I call the vicious downward spiral of sin, sin, and more sin. Let me explain with an example. When I was a young teenager, I deeply desired to be accepted by people. Because I desired this so deeply, I would often make up stories to make myself look good. Of course, the stories were not true, and I would forget what stories I had told to which person. Soon my friends started catching me in my lies. But would I simply confess my sin and 'fess up to my storytelling? Of course not! That would have been too embarrassing. So I lied some more and blamed others to cover up my deceit. Soon I was caught up in a vicious downward spiral of sin, sin, and more sin. I was making a complete fool of myself. The only way out was to quit! I had to see my sin as sin, turn from it, and change my ways.

My story shows an example of a "little sin" that got out of control. However, "bigger sins" can get even more out of control. In my own life, drinking led to sexual immorality. Sexual immorality led to pregnancy outside of marriage. Pregnancy outside of marriage led to abortion. Abortion led to thoughts of suicide.

Do you see how this vicious downward spiral of sin, sin, and more sin can start with just a "little sin" such as telling lies? We like to compare sins to see which is worse—for instance, most of us would consider murder or abortion to be a much bigger sin than a lie. But it is important to note that to God, sin is sin. There are no "little sins" or "big sins." Whether the cud of hurt and pain is self-inflicted sin or sin inflicted by another person which has turned into sin deep within your

The vicious downward spiral of sin, sin, and more sin!

own heart, we must all realize and admit that we are sinners! Until we get to this point, God cannot help us.

Psalm 51:5 is an interesting verse:

> Surely I was sinful at birth, sinful from the time my mother conceived me.

Romans 3:23 confirms this:

> For all have sinned and fall short of the glory of God.

7

According to Romans 3:23, how many people are sinners?

_____

_____

_____

Does that include you and me?

_____

_____

_____

Would you agree with the statement that you are a sinner? Why or why not?

_____

_____

_____

Let's talk about the cud of hurt and pain again. You see, when we stuff or swallow the cud of hurt and pain deep within our hearts—deep within our inmost beings—we do not handle it in the way God intended. When we stuff the cud of hurt and pain deep within, it begins to fester like a wound that hasn't been properly cleansed. As the cud of hurt and pain begins to fester and become infected, it turns into another form that poisons our lives. When a cow chews on grass or cow feed, the food changes form. It does not look

It all gets chewed up together as one big wad of cud!

the same. In fact, it looks pretty gross. The same is true of the cud of our hurt and pain. It takes on a new form—the form of anger and bitterness. Thus, the hurt, pain, anger, and bitterness all get chewed up together as one big wad of cud. This big wad of cud, which we stuff or swallow deep within our hearts, is sin to God. God considers this sin, because we do not handle the hurt, pain, anger, and bitterness in the way He intended.

What is included in this big wad of cud?

_____

_____

_____

Why does God consider this sin?

_____

_____

_____

Psalm 4:4 teaches:

> In your anger do not sin; when you are on your beds, search your hearts and be silent.

Ephesians 4:26 repeats God's warning:

> "In your anger do not sin": Do not let the sun go down while you are still angry.

It is this sin—this big wad of cud that not only includes our hurt and pain but also our anger and bitterness—which causes many cruddy consequences in our lives. To put it simply, cud causes crud! The word *crud* means "any substance considered disgustingly foul or unpleasant."[3] The definition of *consequence* is "the effect, result, or outcome of something occurring earlier."[4] So we could describe *cruddy consequences* as "something disgustingly foul or unpleasant that occurs as a result of something that happened earlier in our lives, which

The vicious downward spiral of sin, sin, and more sin!

then causes the vicious downward spiral of sin, sin, and more sin." This is important, so let me repeat it: When we continue to chew on the cud of hurt and pain, instead of handling it in the manner God intended, it becomes one big wad of cud, which includes anger and bitterness. This is what causes the crud you're going to learn about next.

The following exercise lists a number of cruddy consequences. As you read each consequence, put a √ next to any one that you have seen in your own life. It doesn't matter how frequently you have struggled with it—put a √ if you have ever experienced the consequence in your life. Are you ready? Let's take a look.

Cruddy Consequences

- ❏ Guilt
- ❏ Shame
- ❏ Fear
- ❏ Anxiety—which could also be described as nervousness, worry, or concerns, which can even cause difficulty breathing and/or a rapid heartbeat
- ❏ Avoidance or denial—which means that you either denied you did something wrong, or lied if you were asked about it
- ❏ Blame—which means that you blamed someone else for what you did instead of taking responsibility for your own actions
- ❏ Bad memories
- ❏ Nightmares
- ❏ Depression—including feeling sad for a long time
- ❏ Rage—including outbursts of anger
- ❏ Being overprotective—of yourself and/or your loved ones
- ❏ Relationship difficulties—detaching yourself from friends and family, or choosing bad relationships
- ❏ Self-destructive behaviors—including eating problems or harming yourself (which can include drugs, alcohol, cutting, and/or suicidal thoughts)

Put a √ by any that you have seen in your own life.

11

Have you seen any of these cruddy consequences in your life? Well, there is hope! We will be learning more about cruddy consequences and how to overcome them in chapter 3. Until then, let me prepare you by sharing the following story, told in Luke 7:36–50:

> Now one of the Pharisees invited Jesus to have dinner with him, so he went to the Pharisee's house and reclined at the table. When a woman who had lived a sinful life in that town learned that Jesus was eating at the Pharisee's house, she brought an alabaster jar of perfume, and as she stood behind him at his feet weeping, she began to wet his feet with her tears. Then she wiped them with her hair, kissed them and poured perfume on them.
>
> When the Pharisee who had invited him saw this, he said to himself, "If this man were a prophet, he would know who is touching him and what kind of woman she is—that she is a sinner."
>
> Jesus answered him, "Simon, I have something to tell you."
>
> "Tell me, teacher," he said.
>
> "Two men owned money to a certain money lender. One owed him five hundred denarii, and the other fifty. Neither of them had the money to pay him back, so he canceled the debts of both. Now which of them will love him more?"
>
> Simon replied, "I suppose the one who had the bigger debt canceled."
>
> "You have judged correctly," Jesus said.
>
> Then he turned toward the woman and said to Simon, "Do you see this woman? I came into your house. You did not give me any water for my feet, but she wet my feet with her tears and wiped them with her hair. You did not give me a kiss, but this woman, from the time I entered, has not stopped kissing my feet. You did not put oil on my

head, but she has poured perfume on my feet. Therefore, I tell you, her many sins have been forgiven—for she loved much. But he who has been forgiven little loves little."

Then Jesus said to her, "Your sins are forgiven."

The other guests began to say among themselves, "Who is this who even forgives sins?"

Jesus said to the woman, "Your faith has saved you; go in peace."

The sinful woman was hurting deeply. I am sure she made a lot of mistakes in her life and, as a result, had many of the same cruddy consequences we struggle with today. The Bible doesn't tell us what her sin was, but I am sure that some of her hurt was from self-inflicted sins and some was from sins inflicted by others. Regardless, she was hurting deeply. She knew that Jesus was her only hope. That's why she came to Him. That's why she kneeled at His feet and wept. That's why she anointed His feet with perfume, wiped them with her hair, and kissed them. She knew that Jesus was her only hope.

Our only hope is to be like this sinful woman and admit that we are sinners, and need God's healing. It doesn't matter if the hurt in our heart comes from self-inflicted sin or sin inflicted by another. What matters is what we do with *the sin in our own heart* as a result of that hurt. Once we admit that we are sinners, we can then come to Jesus like the sinful woman and be set free from the cud and the crud! Only then will we get to the place where we can accept Jesus' words like the sinful woman did.

Luke 7:48 and 50 teaches us these wonderful words from Jesus:

Your sins are forgiven. . . . Your faith has saved you; *go in peace* (emphasis added).

13

This is important, so let me repeat it in a slightly different way: no matter what you have done as a result of self-inflicted sin, or what you have been through as a result of sin inflicted by another, God wants you to *go in peace!*

Continue to complete each chapter in this book so that you can *go in peace!* God loves you deeply and desires for you to be set free from the disgusting wad of cud that is made up of hurt, pain, anger, and bitterness, which causes the cruddy consequences of depression, anxiety, and rage (to name just a few). As you are set free from the cud, you will be set free from the cruddy consequences. Never forget: God loves you more than you know! *Go in peace!*

DIGGING DEEPER

In view of God's love, take time this week to look up the following verses which prove the truths you learned in this chapter. Underline or highlight these truths in your Bible. Then write them in a journal or on a 3×5 card so that you will have them close at hand when needed.

You are loved—Jeremiah 31:3; Isaiah 54:10;
    Ephesians 3:17–19
You were created in God's image—Genesis 1:26–27
You are a work of art—Ephesians 2:10
You were knit together in your mother's womb—
    Psalm 139:13–16
You are not a mistake—Psalm 119:73
You are of worth—Luke 12:6–7
You are to go in peace!—Luke 7:48, 50

MISSING THE MARK

In the last chapter, we learned that we are not only loved deeply, but also that we are created in the image and likeness of God. Now we are ready to learn another important truth. Although we were *created* in the image and likeness of God, we were *born* in the image and likeness of Adam. Genesis 5:3 explains:

> When Adam had lived 130 years, he had a son in his *own* likeness, in his *own* image; and he named him Seth (emphasis added).

All of mankind—including you and me—can trace their ancestry back to Adam. Thus, we were *born* in the image and likeness of Adam. This truth affects our lives greatly. Therefore, let's take a look at the story of Adam and Eve.

God created Adam and his wife, Eve, and put them in the Garden of Eden. God provided for all of their needs. However, He had one rule for them to follow:

You must not eat from the tree of the knowledge of good and evil, for when you eat of it you will surely die.

—Genesis 2:17

What was the one rule that Adam and Eve were to follow?

_____

_____

_____

What would happen if they did not follow God's command?

_____

_____

_____

One day, Lucifer (also known by names such as the serpent, Satan, and the devil) came to Eve and said, "Did God really say, 'You must not eat from any tree in the garden'?" (Genesis 3:1). Lucifer is very clever and smart. Although he did not choose to follow God, he knows the Bible really well. Many times, he will twist verses from the Bible to cause confusion. He wants to hurt and destroy us. Not only that, but he also wants to destroy our relationship with God.

In view of this, we need to understand the three steps that entice us and tempt us to sin.

1. Lucifer thinks up the lie.
2. The world sells the lie by enticing us.
3. Our flesh, when we allow ourselves to be tempted to sin, buys the lie.

Let me explain by going back to our story of Adam and Eve. First, Lucifer thought up the lie. He whispered to Eve, "You will not surely die" (Genesis 3:4). He does the same thing to us each day, telling us that sin is not really that bad and will not carry any consequences. Second, Eve saw that the fruit was pleasing to the eye. The world will often try to sell Lucifer's lies by enticing us and making something

Eve saw that the fruit was pleasing to the eye!

look attractive and pleasurable. The world cleverly packages the lie for us to see and then causes us to believe that there is some reason we need what the world is selling. Finally, Eve fell victim to her own fleshly desires when she chose to give in to the temptation. Pay attention to the wording of Genesis 3:6:

> When the woman *saw* that the fruit of the tree was good for food and *pleasing to the eye,* and also *desirable* for gaining wisdom, she took some and ate it (emphasis added).

In the Bible, the word *flesh* sometimes means "the weaker element in [our] human nature."[1] In other words, when we are

She took some and ate it!

living by our flesh, we are choosing to make weaker decisions based on our fleshly *desires* and *feelings,* not on truth or what we know is right.

There is another important point in this story: Adam was with Eve when she decided to eat the forbidden fruit. He didn't stop her, and he didn't try to protect her from following her fleshly desires. In fact, he also

18

ate the forbidden fruit. He fell short of the duties that God had assigned to him. Because of his disobedience, mankind has ever since been plagued with a terrible disease—a disease that has been passed down throughout the generations to you and me. This disease is sin, which results in death.

When Adam and Eve ate the forbidden fruit, they fulfilled the warning of God:

> You must not eat from the tree of knowledge of good and evil, for when you eat of it you will surely die.
>
> —Genesis 2:17

Romans 5:12 teaches:

> When Adam sinned, sin entered the entire human race. Adam's sin brought death, so death spread to everyone, for everyone sinned.
>
> —NLT

According to Romans 5:12, when Adam sinned what happened to the entire human race?

_____

_____

_____

Does that include you?

_____

_____

_____

Remember that even though you were *created* in the image and likeness of God, you were *born* in the image and likeness of Adam. Thus, you were born physically alive but spiritually dead. You did not have the presence of God in your life, or the knowledge of His ways. This brings us to a very important issue: salvation.

In the last chapter, we read the story of the sinful woman. In a few short sentences, Jesus said some amazing things to her. Let's take a look again at what He had to say:

> Then Jesus said to her, "Your sins are forgiven. . . . Your faith has saved you; go in peace."
>
> —Luke 7:48 and 50

In addition to Jesus telling the sinful woman to *go in peace,* He also said that her faith had saved her. Although the sinful woman was born physically alive, she was also born spiritually dead as a result of inheriting the deadly disease of sin from Adam. The same is true for you and me. We were born in the image and likeness of Adam rather than God.[2] We were born with sin present in our physical bodies.[3] We were born with a spirit that is dead to God.[4] We were born under the power and authority of Lucifer.[5] We were born a slave to sin.[6] We were born to suffer physical death.[7] And we were born with an eternal destination: the lake of fire.[8]

But there is wonderful news! In fact, the most wonderful news of all! Although we were born into all of the yuck listed above, we can be reborn or born again. This is also known as "being saved." This is what Jesus meant when He said to the sinful woman, "Your faith has saved you" (Luke 7:50).

Let's learn what Jesus' words mean by looking at another interesting verse. Romans 5:19 states:

> For just as through the disobedience of the one man [Adam] the many were made sinners [including you and

me], so also through the obedience of the one man [Jesus Christ] the many will be made righteous.

Righteous means that we have a right standing before God. The only person who can grant you and me that right standing before God is Jesus Christ, His Son. That is why Jesus could say to the sinful woman, "Your faith has saved you."

The name *Jesus* literally means "the Lord saves,"[9] and the name *Christ* means "the anointed one."[10] Therefore, *Jesus Christ* is the anointed one who saves. He has been with God the Father since the beginning.[11] And though it is difficult for us to understand, God the Father and God the Son are one.[12] In fact, there is only one true God,[13] who by nature is evident in three persons: (1) God the Father, (2) God the Son, and (3) God the Holy Spirit.[14]

The love He has for you is so deep!

While God the Father loves His Son deeply, He loves you as well. In fact, the love He has for you is so deep that He sacrificed His Son, Jesus Christ, to give you eternal life. And because the Son also loves you, He willingly gave up His life to save yours. But the miracle of all miracles is that on the third day following His death, He physically rose from the grave.[15] *Physically* means that Christ rose in bodily form from the grave. He appeared to more than 500 eyewitnesses after His resurrection[16] and then ascended to heaven, where He sits today at the right hand of God the Father.[17]

Through His resurrection, Jesus proved that if you, too, become born again, you will also have eternal life and will be set free from all the yuck into which you were born. This is why Jesus had the power and authority to say to the sinful woman, "Your faith has saved you."

Has your faith saved you? Have you been born again?

_____

_____

_____

If so, when did you become born again? How did it happen?

_____

_____

_____

If not, do you want to accept Jesus Christ as your Lord and Savior right now?

_____

_____

_____

Romans 10:9–10 teaches the following:

> If you confess with your mouth Jesus as Lord, and believe in your heart that God raised Him from the dead, you will be saved; for with the heart a person believes, resulting in righteousness, and with the mouth he confesses, resulting in salvation.
>
> —NASB

If you haven't accepted Jesus Christ as your Lord and Savior and you want to do so, it is as easy as this verse says! Simply confess with your mouth that Jesus is Lord and believe in your heart that God raised Him from the dead. You can pray a prayer like this from your heart:

Dear God, I know that I am a sinner. I know I cannot save myself. I ask for Your forgiveness for the things that I have done wrong. Lord, please help me to change my sinful ways. I believe Jesus is God. I know that You, Jesus, died on the cross for me so that my sins could be washed away. I believe that You rose from the dead to live through me. I now receive You, Jesus, as my Lord and Savior. I accept Your offer of forgiveness and eternal life. Lord, I thank You for the wonderful and free gift that You have given to me! In Jesus' precious name, Amen.

Pray a prayer from your heart!

If you have no desire to accept Jesus Christ as your Lord and Savior at this time, I encourage you to continue working through this book. Do not stop! However, you need to realize that not all of the promises of God will apply to you. What you learned in chapters 1 and 2 will apply—God loves you, and you are not a mistake. But the additional promises from this point forward will only apply to those who have accepted Jesus as their Lord and Savior. If at any time you decide to accept Christ into your life, simply pray the prayer that is written here. At that moment, *all* of the promises of God will be yours!

Now, when we accept the freedom that Jesus Christ gives, we need to realize that Satan will begin to wage a battle against us. This is a battle in the spiritual realm that cannot be seen, but it includes you and me. This is why we will struggle with the three things we learned about at the beginning of this chapter: (1) Lucifer, (2) the world, and (3) the flesh. Let's learn more about Lucifer and the sin he so badly wants us to bite into.

There is pleasure in sin for a short season!

Lucifer was created by God and was considered the most beautiful of all the angels. In fact, the Bible tells us that he was "the model of perfection, full of wisdom and perfect in beauty" (Ezekiel 28:12). The Bible goes on to say that he was blameless in all his ways from the day he was created until wickedness was found in him.[18] It was at this moment that Lucifer became known as Satan. The wickedness found in Satan was *not of God*. In human beings, this wickedness is called *sin*. Sin is a lack of perfection. It is important to remember that *sin is not of God*.[19]

What is wickedness called in human beings?

_____

_____

_____

Is wickedness or sin of God?

_____

_____

_____

Deuteronomy 32:4 tells us more about God:

He is the Rock, his works are perfect, and all his ways are just. A faithful God who does no wrong, upright and just is he.

We learn from this verse that God's works are perfect. He is just in all His ways. He is faithful, upright and can do no wrong. What all this means is that there is only good in God. Therefore, wickedness and sin are *not* of Him.

Now, with Satan's wickedness came pride. He wanted to be above all things. He wanted the place of honor that belongs only to God. He wanted to sit on God's throne and rule over all. He wanted God's authority and power. In fact, he wanted to be just like God.[20] Isaiah 14:13–14 shows what Satan had to say:

I will ascend to heaven; *I will* raise my throne above the stars of God; *I will* sit enthroned on the mount of assembly, on the utmost heights of the sacred mountain. *I will* ascend above the tops of the clouds; *I will* make myself like the Most High (emphasis added).

We must be careful not to become like Satan. We need to pay attention to "I, I, I" when we speak, because we can also become prideful like Satan. The Bible teaches that pride goes before a fall![21] In other words, we, too, can fall when we become prideful.

As a result of Satan's pride and rebellion, he was kicked out of heaven along with one-third of the angels who followed him. When they were kicked out of heaven, they became known as fallen angels (or demons) and were hurled down to earth. Revelation 12:9 teaches:

The great dragon was hurled down—that ancient serpent called the devil, or Satan, who leads the whole world astray. He was hurled [sent] to the earth, and his angels with him.

Who was kicked out of heaven?

_____

_____

_____

Where was he hurled?

_____

_____

_____

Who was with him?

_____

_____

_____

Now, there is another important truth found within the above verse: "Satan, who leads the whole world astray." "The whole world" includes you and me. The wrong choices we make lead us astray!

Each day, there are choices we must make—wise choices and foolish choices. Adam and Eve had a choice: They could choose to follow God and the one rule that He gave them, or they could choose to be led astray by the lies of Satan and the desires of their flesh. Unfortunately for you and me, they chose to be led astray by the lies of Satan and follow their fleshly desires.

Choices—so many choices!

We are just like Adam and Eve. We were born in the image and likeness of Adam, and thus we have Adam's sinful nature. This is why many times we make wrong and foolish choices. As we read in the last chapter, "All have sinned and fall short of the glory of God" (Romans 3:23). Remember, this includes you and me.

The word *sin* in the Greek (the language in which part of the Bible was written) literally means "to miss the mark."[22] Back in biblical times, men would use bows and arrows for hunting and for warfare. To be the best they could be with their bows and arrows, they would have to do a lot of target practice. If their arrow missed the mark during practice (or, in other words, they missed the center of the bull's-eye), they would call this *sin*.

Sin means to miss the mark!

The same is true for you and me today. When we miss the mark—in other words, miss making wise choices that are pleasing to God—we sin. Sin includes our wrong actions, our wrong attitudes, and our wrong thoughts.[23] It also includes what we talked about in the last chapter—the big wad of cud of hurt, pain, anger, and bitterness we choose to swallow and stuff deep within our heart, deep within our inmost being, which then causes such cruddy consequences as depression, anxiety, and rage.

In 1 John 1:8, we read:

> If we claim to be without sin, *we deceive ourselves* and the truth is not in us (emphasis added).

But there is wonderful news for all who have accepted Jesus as their Lord and Savior. As John 1:12–13 says:

> To all who received him, to those who believed in his name, he gave the right to become *children of God*—children born not of natural descent, nor of human decision or a husband's will, but born of God (emphasis added).

If you have accepted Jesus Christ as your Lord and Savior, you are God's child. He doesn't want you to stay in the vicious downward spiral of sin, sin, and more sin that leads to the miry pit. He has made a way to lift you out of that pit of sin, but it requires you to make a choice.

Faith choices or flesh choices!

Each day we make choices—faith choices or flesh choices. A *faith choice* is a wise choice we make according to the truth of God's Word. A *flesh choice*, on the other hand, is a foolish choice that we make based on our fleshly desires and/or feelings, such as our lusts or emotions. It is best for us to make the faith choice, because it is only by the faith choice that we will be set free!

Romans 8:1 shares a wonderful truth:

> There is therefore now no condemnation to those who are in Christ Jesus, who do not walk according to the flesh, but according to the Spirit.
>
> —NKJV

The word *condemnation* in this verse means "to judge worthy of punishment."[24] Even though we were born in the image and likeness of Adam, we avoided the punishment of God the moment we accepted Jesus Christ as our Lord and Savior. That's why the verse says that there is now "no condemnation" to those who are "in Christ Jesus."

But it gets even better! Even though we were born slaves to sin, we now have the ability to walk according to the Spirit of God. As we make wise faith choices based on the Word of God, we walk according to the Spirit. Therefore, it is important for us to always *think* before we choose to do something and not make rash or foolish choices. *Rash* means to be hasty in decisions, choices, actions, and/or speech. It also means to not consider the consequences.[25] When we make rash or foolish choices, we walk according to the flesh. When we walk according to the flesh, there are always consequences. (We will learn more about these consequences in the next chapter.)

As you continue to read this book, remember that you have the power of God in your life and can walk differently from the world and the flesh. You don't have to act on your feelings or desires, but can choose to take the time to think and make wise choices according to the Spirit of God. You can choose to be wise. Allow the truth of who you are in Christ—you are saved; you are God's child; you are free from condemnation—to equip you to make wise choices. As you do this, you will walk according to the Spirit of God.

In the next two chapters, be prepared to learn how to get rid of the cud and the crud that you learned about in chapter 1. Until then, remember that there is hope! God loves you more than you know! He desires you to learn all so that you can *go in peace!*

DIGGING DEEPER

Take time this week to look up the following verses that prove the truth you learned in this chapter. Underline or highlight these verses in your Bible. Then write them in a journal or on a 3×5 card so that you will have them close at hand when you need encouragement.

You are saved—Titus 3:5
You are His child—Psalm 68:5; John 1:12–13;
   Romans 8:14–15; 1 John 3:1
You are free from condemnation—Romans 8:1

CHAPTER THREE

DO NOT BE DECEIVED

In chapter 1, we discussed some interesting tidbits about the eating habits of the cow. We learned that when we stuff and swallow our hurts deep within our hearts, we become like a cow as we chew on the cud of our hurt, pain, anger, and bitterness. Now let's look at more of the cruddy consequences that come as a result of chewing the cud. Galatians 6:7 warns:

> Don't be misled. Remember that you can't ignore God and get away with it. You will always *reap* what you *sow!*
>
> —NLT, emphasis added

Sowing and reaping are words that come from farming. To *sow* means "to plant seeds for growing."[1] To *reap* means "to harvest a crop [from what was sown]."[2] In other words, if you were to sow a sunflower seed (and you took proper care of it), in a few weeks you would have an abundance of sunflower

You will reap what you sow!

seeds that you could reap and harvest.

There is a direct relationship between sowing and reaping. If you sow corn, you will reap corn. If you sow sunflower seeds, you will reap sunflower seeds. Corn does not grow from sunflower seeds, and sunflowers do not grow from corn. Likewise, what you sow in life will determine what you reap in life. Wise choices will reap good consequences, while foolish choices will reap bad consequences. Remember, as we discussed in chapter 1, the word *consequence* means "the effect, result, or outcome of something occurring earlier."[3]

It is true; there are consequences! You will reap what you sow! Sometimes you will see the results of your choices immediately. For example, when you choose to go to work and do a good job for your boss, you will reap a good consequence by getting paid. When you choose not to study for an upcoming test, you may reap a bad consequence by failing the exam. Consequences are the effect, result, or outcome of something that occurred earlier.

Many times, you will not immediately see the results of what you sow. The consequences that you have reaped in your life can appear months or even years later. For example, years of smoking can result in the bad consequence of getting lung cancer. On the other hand, studying medicine for years can result in the good consequence of becoming a doctor. Each consequence came after many years of sowing either foolish or wise choices.

Beware! Don't be fooled into thinking that you will not reap the consequences of foolish choices, even if at first it seems that you have gotten away with it. You will always reap what you sow. There is no getting around it.

There will be consequences when you choose to chew on the cud of your hurt, pain, anger, and bitterness. So let's talk about the cruddy consequences that we looked at briefly in chapter 1. Remember the list of these cruddy consequences: guilt, shame, fear, anxiety, avoidance, denial, blame, bad memories, nightmares, depression, rage, over-protectiveness, relationship difficulties, and self-destructive behaviors.

Proverbs 22:8 states,

> He who sows wickedness reaps trouble.

In chapter 2, we discussed that wickedness in human beings is called *sin*. Proverbs 22:8 could therefore read, "He who sows *sin* reaps trouble." In chapter 1, we also looked at how the cud of hurt and pain changes into one big wad of cud, which includes anger and bitterness, as we continue to chew on it. Stuffing or swallowing this anger and bitterness deep within our hearts is sin to God. This is true even if the anger and bitterness comes as a result of sin inflicted on us by another, because God never intended for us to chew and swallow our anger and bitterness. We could therefore take Proverbs 22:8 and apply it to our lives by saying it this way: "He who sows *sin* [the *sin* of chewing on their cud of hurt, pain, anger, and bitterness] reaps trouble [the trouble of cruddy consequences]."

God never intended for us to chew the cud!

So, the bottom line is this: If we choose to chew on the cud of hurt, pain, anger, and bitterness, and don't give it to God in the manner He intended, we will reap the cruddy consequences. This is so important to understand that I am going to repeat it again. As I do, underline it:

> If we choose to chew on the cud of hurt, pain, anger, and bitterness, and don't give it to God in the manner He intended, we will reap the cruddy consequences.

In view of this truth, let's look more closely at the cruddy consequences in our lives. (Remember, knowledge is the beginning of freedom!)

The first two cruddy consequences are *guilt* and *shame*. God often uses guilt and shame in our lives to draw us closer to Him. He wants us to be honest with ourselves. He knows that the cruddy consequences will hurt us and those around us. *Guilt* means "a feeling of responsibility for wrongdoing."[4] Many times, guilt results from self-inflicted sin, a reaping of our own foolish choices and actions.

In Psalm 38:4, King David expressed the weight of the guilt he felt as a result of his own sin when he wrote,

> My guilt has overwhelmed me like a burden too heavy to bear.

Although we may try to ignore our feelings of guilt as a result of our sin, we cannot escape it, no matter how hard we try. Jeremiah 2:22 describes it this way:

> "Although you wash yourself with soda and use an abundance of soap, the stain of your guilt is still before me," declares the Sovereign LORD.

Psalm 69:5 states it even more clearly:

> You know my folly, O God; my guilt is not hidden from you.

What is your folly? What are some of the things you have done which have caused you to feel guilt?

_____

_____

_____

Shame, on the other hand, means "a painful emotion caused by a strong sense of guilt, embarrassment, unworthiness or disgrace."[5] From this definition, we see that shame can result from self-inflicted sin or sin inflicted by another. Psalm 44:15 describes shame in this manner:

> My disgrace is before me all day long, and my face is covered with shame.

What are some of the things that have caused you shame?

_____

_____

_____

Let's go back to the story of Adam and Eve that we first looked at in chapter 2 to learn more about the cruddy consequences. It is interesting to see that even Adam and Eve reaped the consequences of their sin:

> The LORD God said, "It is not good for the man to be alone. I will make a helper suitable for him. . . ." Then the

LORD God made a woman from the rib he had taken out of the man, and he brought her to the man.

The man said, "This is now bone of my bones and flesh of my flesh; she shall be called 'woman,' for she was taken out of man."

For this reason a man will leave his father and mother and be united to his wife, and they will become one flesh.

The man and his wife were both naked, and they felt no shame.

Now the serpent was more crafty than any of the wild animals the LORD God had made. He said to the woman, "Did God really say, 'You must not eat from any tree in the garden'?"

The woman said to the serpent, "We may eat fruit from the trees in the garden, but God did say, 'You must not eat fruit from the tree that is in the middle of the garden, and you must not touch it, or you will die.'"

"You will not surely die," the serpent said to the woman. "For God knows that when you eat of it your eyes will be opened, and you will be like God, knowing good and evil."

When the woman saw that the fruit of the tree was good for food and pleasing to the eye, and also desirable for gaining wisdom, she took some and ate it. She also gave some to her husband, who was with her, and he ate it.

Then the eyes of both of them were opened, and they realized they were naked; so they sewed fig leaves together and made coverings for themselves.

Then the man and his wife heard the sound of the LORD God as he was walking in the garden in the cool of the day, and they hid from the LORD God among the trees of the garden. But the LORD God called to the man, "Where are you?"

He answered, "I heard you in the garden, and I was afraid because I was naked; so I hid."

And he said, "Who told you that you were naked? Have you eaten from the tree that I commanded you not to eat from?"

The man said, "The woman you put here with me—she gave me some fruit from the tree, and I ate it."

Then the LORD God said to the woman, "What is this you have done?"

The woman said, "The serpent deceived me, and I ate."

—Genesis 2:18, 22–3:13

They fell into the vicious downward spiral of sin, sin, and more sin!

Don't overlook the fact that before Adam and Eve ate the fruit, they had no *shame*. The reason? Because they had no *sin* in their lives at that moment. When we are in God's perfect will, there is no guilt and no shame. However, the moment we step out of His will, we experience both guilt and shame and, even worse, many other cruddy consequences. Unfortunately for Adam and Eve, this condition of having no sin in their lives changed. As the story of Adam and Eve unfolded, they fell into the vicious downward spiral of sin, sin, and more sin.

In Genesis 3:1, Satan asked Eve,

Did God really say, "You must not eat from any tree in the garden"?

The enemy *always* takes the truth of God's Word and twists it just enough to cause us to doubt. As a result of Satan's enticing lies, Adam and Eve fell into temptation when they chose to disobey God's command. Genesis 3:6 shows the moment when sin entered into their lives:

> When the woman saw that the fruit of the tree was good
> for food and pleasing to the eye, and also desirable for
> gaining wisdom, she took some and ate it. She also gave
> some to her husband, who was with her, and he ate it.

Adam and Eve sinned the moment they *chose* to eat the fruit
because they *chose* to disobey the one rule that God had given
to them.

When did sin enter Adam and Eve's lives?

_____

_____

_____

What made this a sin?

_____

_____

_____

It is true that Adam and Eve sinned when they chose to
eat the fruit. However, I believe that the sin in their hearts
began when they took a second look at the fruit. Pay careful
attention to the wording of Genesis 3:6:

> When the woman *saw* that the fruit of the tree was good
> for food and *pleasing to the eye,* and also *desirable* for gain-
> ing wisdom, she took some and ate it (emphasis added).

The sin began when Eve *saw* that the fruit was good.

The word *saw,* as it appears in the original language, could
actually be translated "to gaze at, to look intently at, to observe, to consider, to learn about, and to give attention to."[6]

Sin begins with the second look!

In fact, the tense of the word *saw* in this verse indicates that it relates "not so much as to one occasion, [but] as to a continued condition . . . frequent repetition."[7] In other words, Eve gazed at the fruit and considered eating it for some time. When she *saw* that the fruit was good, it means that she took more than a causal glance—she *chose* to gaze at it and then consider and think about eating it.

This is also where sin begins for us: the second look. Sin first takes root when we begin to look at something intently and consider doing wrong. When we take that second look, sin begins in our minds and our hearts, well before any action has taken place. If we don't stop our thoughts, this can be the beginning of the vicious downward spiral of sin, sin, and more sin.

So be warned. Be careful about what you look at and what you think about.

Let's continue with the story of Adam and Eve to see what cruddy consequences they experienced as a result of their sin:

> Then the eyes of both of them were opened, and they realized they were *naked;* so they sewed fig leaves together and made *coverings* for themselves. Then the man and his wife heard the sound of the LORD God as he was walking in the garden in the cool of the day, and they *hid* from the LORD God among the trees of the garden. But the LORD God called to the man, "Where are you?" He answered, "I heard you in the garden, and I was *afraid* because I was *naked;* so I *hid.*"
>
> —Genesis 3:7–10, emphasis added

Naked means that Adam and Eve felt exposed because of their sin. They knew that they would get caught for what they had done wrong, so they immediately sewed fig leaves together to try to cover themselves. But that wasn't enough. It didn't make them feel any better. In fact, they were afraid. When they heard God walking in the garden, they tried to hide from Him. In addition to the guilt and shame, they immediately reaped the cruddy consequences of *fear* and *anxiety*. They also tried to avoid and deny their wrongdoing by covering themselves and hiding—two more of the cruddy consequences of sin also known as *avoidance* and *denial*.

What cruddy consequences did Adam and Eve immediately experience? (Hint: list the four words in italics [except naked] in the paragraph above.)

_____

_____

_____

There are always consequences to sin. If you are unsure of whether you have ever experienced any of these cruddy consequences associated with sin, let me explain it this way. If you have done something wrong, you may struggle with *fear* that your sin will be found out, *fear* that something bad will happen, *fear* that nothing good will ever happen . . . *fear, fear, FEAR!*

You may also suffer from anxiety. *Anxiety* means abnormal uneasiness, worry, and fear that is often accompanied by physical signs such as sweating and a rapid heartbeat.[8] This especially occurs when you are reminded of the deep heart hurt—the original event that began the cud chewing.

You may also experience the cruddy consequences of avoidance and denial. For instance, you may *avoid* the area or place that reminds you of the sin or hurtful event. Or you may *deny* that the sin affects you in any way and tell yourself: *so-and-so did this, but it was no big deal. I can handle it.*

Have you ever experienced fear, anxiety, avoidance, and/or denial?

If so, which ones?

Jeremiah 23:24 teaches an important truth:

> "Can anyone *hide* in secret places so that I cannot see him?" declares the LORD. "Do not I fill heaven and earth?" (emphasis added).

We cannot hide from God! He sees all and He knows all. And He wants us to get rid of the sin in our hearts so that we can be washed clean. This was true for Adam and Eve, and it's true for you and me as well. God uses the consequences to draw us to Him. He wants us to deal with the deep heart hurts.

In Genesis 3:11–13, God asked several questions of Adam and Eve to get them thinking about the sin they had committed:

"Who told you that you were naked? Have you eaten from the tree that I commanded you not to eat from?"

The man said, "The woman you put here with me—she gave me some fruit from the tree, and I ate it."

Then the LORD God said to the woman, "What is this you have done?"

The woman said, "The serpent deceived me, and I ate."

Do you see how Adam and Eve blamed others to try and get the guilt off of themselves? Adam blamed both Eve and God for his own actions. Eve blamed the serpent for deceiving her. *Blame* is another cruddy consequence of sin that we encounter as we go deeper into the vicious downward spiral of sin, sin, and more sin.

Do you ever try to blame others for your actions?

_____

_____

_____

When you blame others, does God consider this sin?

_____

_____

_____

Can you get away with your sin, or will God find you out?

_____

_____

_____

Spins out of control!

The longer you and I try to deny feelings or actions associated with our sin, the longer we will reap the cruddy consequences. Trying to hide our sinful behavior from God by denying, avoiding, and blaming others only creates fear and anxiety in our lives. Can you see how this becomes a vicious downward spiral of sin, sin, and more sin? First John 1:6 and 8 explains it this way:

> If we claim to have fellowship with him [God] yet walk in the darkness, we lie and do not live by the truth. . . . If we claim to be without sin, *we deceive ourselves* and the truth is not in us (emphasis added).

As we deceive ourselves, the vicious downward spiral of sin, sin, and more sin spins out of control and we start to experience the additional cruddy consequences of bad memories, nightmares, and depression.

Lamentations 3:19–20 states,

> I remember my affliction and my wandering, the bitterness and the gall. I well remember them, and my soul is downcast within me.

Bad memories can come when we least expect them. They can be triggered by something as simple as a song, a flower, a smell, a certain time of year, or even a certain type of clothing. It is as if the memories were always there, lurking, waiting to return when we least expect them.

Nightmares are dreams that remind us of the sin or hurtful event. Usually, the nightmare is the same dream repeated over and over for a long period of time. Many times, our nightmares involve danger to ourself or our loved ones whom we are unable to help.

Depression is another cruddy consequence that we may experience as a result of not dealing with a deep heart hurt in the manner God intended. Depression is basically a prolonged state of feeling sad.[9] Depression will typically continue until we are willing to deal with the root reason of the cud in our lives. This means that it will continue until we stop chewing, stuffing, and swallowing the original hurt and pain that we chewed up into one big wad of cud, which includes anger and bitterness.

Have you struggled with bad memories, nightmares, or depression?

_____

_____

_____

If so, which ones?

_____

_____

_____

Bad memories, nightmares, and depression can trigger other cruddy consequences in our lives, such as *rage, over-protectiveness, relationship difficulties,* and/or *self-destructive behaviors.*

Rage means "to be furiously angry, [and/or] to continue out of control."[10] In other words, rage could be described as uncontrollable outbursts of anger.

Over-protectiveness is a heightened state of always being on the alert for danger. If you struggle with this cruddy consequence, you may feel as if someone is always out to get you. You become over-protective of yourself and/or your loved ones.

Relationship difficulties could best be described as a detachment from friends, family, and other loved ones. If you suffer from this cruddy consequence, you may sabotage good friendships and hang out with people who are a bad influence on you in order to reinforce your feelings of unworthiness.

Self-destructive behaviors are any type of actions that have a negative affect on a person's life. These can include behaviors such as over-eating, over-sleeping, over-cleaning, over-spending, or over-anything. They can also include the opposite, such as under-eating, under-sleeping, under-cleaning, or under-anything. Many people develop eating disorders such as anorexia and/or bulimia. Many turn to drugs and/or alcohol as a means to numb the deep heart hurt. Some even go so far as to cut or harm themselves, just to feel something or as means of punishing themselves. Other self-destructive behaviors can include suicidal thoughts or suicide attempts.

Is rage, over-protectiveness, relationship difficulties, or self-destructive behavior (such as anorexia, bulimia, cutting or harming yourself, drugs, alcohol, or suicidal thoughts) a part of your life?

_____

_____

_____

If so, which ones?

_____

_____

_____

Do you see what happens when we don't give the hurt and pain to God? Do you see how we can get caught in the vicious downward spiral of sin, sin, and more sin as we continue to chew on the cud? The sad thing is that when we are in the vicious downward spiral of sin, sin, and more sin, we not only hurt ourselves, but also those around us. Perhaps this is why King David wrote the following when he was broken over his sin:

> My friends and companions avoid me because of my wounds; my neighbors stay far away.
> —Psalm 38:11

In chapter 1, we discussed how deep hurt within our hearts can make it difficult to believe the truth of God's Word when it says that we are loved. It is as if this deep hurt causes such a scaring on the outside of our hearts that we don't allow the truth of God's love to penetrate to the inside of our hearts. It is as if our hearts are covered by a big, thick, disgusting scab and scar tissue. Worse yet, our hearts are not only covered by scabs and scar tissue but are also infected deeply within, which poisons our whole lives.

If this infection of sin (the big wad of cud) is allowed to fester, it can explode like a volcano. This may be seen in the more obvious fit of rage, but it can also explode in fits of depression, over-protectiveness, relationship difficulties, and/ or self-destructive behaviors. When we allow these things to

Explodes like a volcano!

happen, we hurt others around us. Think about it: do you enjoy being around someone who is depressed? What about someone who is yelling all the time in rage? Or, worse yet, someone who is not himself or herself because of drugs or alcohol? Do you see how the cud and infection in our hearts hurts not only us but also those around us? It is as if we are spurting the cud and crud of our sinful behavior like a volcano.

If you cut your finger and do not wash it correctly, the injury will become infected and start to poison your body. If the infection is allowed to fester, it will become filled with pus and other yuck. Then, if you happen to slam your finger in the door, all that pus and poisonous infection will spurt out all over the place. If somebody were standing next to you, they might even get some of the disgusting pus on him or her. Yuck! That is just plain gross!

Just in case you need another gross word picture, let's go back to our story of the cow. Remember, a cow is a cud-chewing animal. As we discussed in chapter 1, cud means "food brought up into the mouth by some animals [such as cows] from the rumen [a part of their stomach] to be chewed again."[11] So, in other words, *cud* is a gross wad of grass or cow feed that has been chewed up, swallowed, burped up, re-chewed, re-swallowed, re-burped up, and chewed on some more.

Notice in the definition above that it says "some animals [such as a cow]." In fact, there are some other cud-chewing animals, one of which is the camel. Camels "eat by swallowing their food whole and allowing it to be partially digested by the stomachs before being chewed as cud later."[12] An interesting fact to know about camels is that when they are in distress, they will spit out a noxious stream of their stomach contents. In fact, the San Diego Zoo claims that "[camels] aren't actually spitting—it's more like throwing up! They bring up the contents of their stomachs, along with saliva, and project it out. This is meant to surprise, distract, or bother whatever the camel feels is threatening it."[13] Isn't that gross?

They aren't actually spitting— it's more like throwing up!

The cud and crud in our lives can also cause us to become offensive to others. People may not want to be around us because they fear that we will throw up and spit depression, rage, over-protectiveness, relationship difficulties, and/or self-destructive behaviors all over them. Even worse, the cruddy consequences are sin to God. Do you see how you and I can become not only like a cow, but also like a camel?

Are you like a camel? Which cruddy consequences do you throw up and spit on others? Circle any of the following cruddy consequences that are in your life:

guilt	shame	fear	anxiety
avoidance	denial	blame	bad memories
nightmares	depression	rage	over-protectiveness
relationship difficulties		self destructive behaviors:	
anorexia/bulimia	drugs/alcohol	cutting/suicidal thoughts	

Note: If you struggle with any of these cruddy consequences and want more information about them, see appendix 1 titled "Cruddy Consequences" in the appendix section in the back of the book.

Do you want to be washed clean from all the cruddy consequences?

_____

_____

_____

In Ezekiel 36:25–26, the Lord promises:

> I will sprinkle clean water on you, and you will be clean; I will cleanse you from all your impurities and from all your idols. I will give you a new heart and put a new spirit in you; I will remove from you your heart of stone and give you a heart of flesh.

In this verse, the word *flesh* does not mean the fleshly desires of our sinful nature as we learned in chapter 2. In this case, the word *flesh* means the soft parts of a body, such as muscular tissue.[14] Therefore, what this verse is saying is that God will heal our broken hearts. He will remove the infection that has caused our hearts to become hard. He will

A heart of flesh!

give us a new heart—one that is soft and pliable and moldable. He will give us a heart that is moldable, so that He can remold and remake us to become all that He intends for us to be. This is what it means to have a heart of flesh. So in other words, the verse could read, "I will remove from you your heart of stone [your heart hardened by the infection of hurt, pain, anger, and bitterness] and give you a heart of flesh [a new heart that is soft, pliable, and moldable, so that you can be all that God intends you to be]."

So how can we be washed clean and receive a new heart? We've already learned that God uses guilt and shame in our lives to draw us to Him. He wants us to be honest with ourselves. Look at what Psalm 83:16 says:

> Cover their faces with shame so that men will seek your name, O LORD.

Although guilt and shame can be some of the cruddy consequences that come as a result of the sin (the cud) in our hearts, God uses these cruddy consequences to cause us to want His help. Just like the verse says: "Cover their faces with shame *so that men will seek your name, O LORD*" (emphasis added).

So how do you and I seek His name so that we can be washed clean from all the cud and cruddy consequences? Psalm 32:5 teaches,

> Then *I acknowledged my sin to you* and did not cover up my iniquity (emphasis added).

As we acknowledge and admit our sins, God will wash us clean and give us a new heart. By circling the cruddy consequences you have struggled with, you have admitted your sin of consequence-spitting. You were being honest with yourself. That's what God desires of you. Now it is time to take the next step: confess.

First John 1:9 tells us how:

> If we confess our sins, he is faithful and just and will forgive us our sins and purify us from all unrighteousness.

To *confess* means "to acknowledge one's sins to God."[15] You admitted your sins to yourself—now take the time to pray and confess them to God. Confess your sin of consequence-spitting and ask Him to forgive you. The moment you confess your sins, God is faithful to forgive.

There is one more thing you must do in addition to admitting and confessing your sin, and that is to repent. *Repent* means to feel such sorrow for your sin—your cruddy consequence-spitting—that you desire to change your life for the better.[16] It is like doing a U-turn. You know that you are heading in the wrong direction with your foolish choices and sin, so you decide to turn around and head in the right direction by making the wise choice to change your ways. This is what it means to *repent*. As you do this, God's Word becomes real in your life. You will no longer be covered with shame.

Repent! Change your ways!

Psalm 34:5 promises,

> Those who look to him are radiant; their faces are *never covered with shame* (emphasis added).

I pray that you will look to God, make the wise choice to follow Him and then change your ways, if needed. It is as easy as 1, 2, 3: (1) admit, (2) confess, and (3) repent. So take a quiet time with God. Admit your failings and sins to yourself. Confess them to God. Then repent by changing your ways. If you do, your face will never be covered by shame.

Have you admitted, confessed, and repented of your sin of cruddy consequence-spitting? If so, know that you are forgiven. You are purified. You are washed clean. Now, you can live by the truth of God's Word, which will cause you to be radiant in His sight.

May your face never be covered with shame. Instead, may you *go in peace!*

DIGGING DEEPER

Spend some quiet time with God. As you do, admit your failings and sins to yourself and then confess them to God. As you confess your sins, take a moment to write them out as a prayer to the Lord. For example, you could pray the following:

> *Lord, I've not trusted You when I am afraid. I realize that worry and anxiety are the opposite of faith, which is unpleasing to You. Blaming others is not taking responsibility for my own actions. Depression is not being content with the many blessings that You have provided. Raging is hurting others around me. Relationship difficulties are not treating others with the respect that is pleasing to You. And self-destructive behaviors are simply wrong, because my body is the temple of the Holy Spirit.*

Once you admit and confess your sin of cruddy consequence-spitting, remember to repent. In other words, change your ways! Stop the cruddy consequence-spitting.

This week, look up the following verses that prove the truth you learned in this chapter. Underline or highlight these truths in your Bible. Then write them in a journal or on a 3×5 card so that you will have them close at hand when you need encouragement.

You are purified—Titus 2:11–14; 1 John 1:9
You are washed clean—Isaiah 1:18; Ezekiel 36:25
You are radiant—Psalm 34:5

CHAPTER FOUR

FORGIVEN AND SET FREE

In the last chapter, we learned that when we admit our sin of cruddy consequence-spitting and confess our sins to God,

> He is faithful and just and will forgive us our sins and purify us from all unrighteousness.
>
> —1 John 1:9

This is true. God faithfully forgives us the moment we confess our sin. However, many times we don't *feel* forgiven. Why is that?

We need to learn that there are other sins chewed up in the big wad of cud. These sins must also be given to God by admitting, confessing, and repenting of them. If these sins are not given to Him, we will end up back in the vicious downward spiral of sin, sin, and more sin, which will again bring us to the place of cruddy consequence-spitting! Therefore, let's learn about these other sins so that we can be set free.

Have you ever had an argument with someone and kept replaying it over in your mind? As you replay it over and over again, you begin to think, *I wish I had said this* or *I wish I had done that.* As you continue to dwell on the argument, you may even begin to replay it in your mind and insert what you *wished* you had said. When you do this, you are not only chewing the cud of hurt and pain, but in your mind you are also beginning to *change the facts* of what really took place.

The element of deception is hidden within the cud!

Many who have become like a cow and a camel by chewing the cud of their hurt and pain feel as if God cannot forgive them. The reason? Because along with the cud of hurt, pain, anger, and bitterness, there is another element contained within the big wad of cud: the element of deception. *Deception* means "a misleading falsehood or a misrepresentation."[1] *Misrepresentation* means "representing the facts incorrectly or falsely."[2]

Remember, as we chew on the cud, it changes form. As we continue to chew on the cud, we can even begin to incorrectly or falsely misrepresent the facts to *ourselves.* In fact, we do this every time we replay the argument in our minds. This is why, as we continue to chew on our cud, we don't feel forgiven and feel we must continue to ask God over and over again to forgive us for our terrible sin. We still do not feel free; there is no peace in our hearts because *an element of deception* is keeping us from admitting the anger we hold in our hearts toward another.

Isaiah 59 holds some interesting tidbits about this deception. Throughout this chapter, we will be taking a look at some of what Isaiah 59 teaches so that we can learn how to be set free and to know without a doubt that we are forgiven—no matter what we may feel. Isaiah 59:1–2 explains:

> Surely the arm of the LORD is not too short to save, nor his ear too dull to hear. But your iniquities have separated you from your God; your sins have hidden his face from you, so that he will not hear.

In chapters 1 and 2, we discussed how it is *sin* to God when we continue to chew on the cud of hurt, pain, anger, and bitterness. Now, while it is true that God forgives us when we confess the sin of consequence-spitting to Him, because of the element of deception, the big wad of cud continues to grow and changes form. It becomes even more disgusting to God, because "we deceive ourselves and the truth is not in us" (1 John

Our sin of deceiving ourselves separates us from God!

1:8). As a result, the vicious downward spiral of sin, sin, and more sin begins anew, again bringing with it all the cruddy consequence-spitting. It is this sin of cud-chewing, including the element of deception, which separates us from God and deprives us of peace. In other words, we could rewrite Isaiah 59:1–2 to say:

> Surely the arm of the LORD is not too short to save [you from your hurt and pain], nor his ear too dull to hear [every

prayer you have prayed]. But your iniquities [of cud chewing, including the element of deception] have separated you from your God; your sins [of cruddy consequence-spitting] have hidden his face from you, so that he will not hear [your prayers, which will cause you to feel unforgiven and deprived of peace].

Our sin of cud-chewing and cruddy consequence-spitting separates us from God! Why? Because we didn't give *everything* to God in the manner He intended. *Everything* includes the element of deception.

What separates us from God?

_____

_____

_____

Why?

_____

_____

_____

This is so important for us to learn and understand. When we don't give the big wad of cud of hurt, pain, anger, and bitterness—which includes the element of deception—to God in the manner He intended, it is as if we have built a brick wall between ourself and Him. Isaiah 59:10 explains it this way:

We have built a wall between ourselves and God!

Like the blind we grope along the wall.

We cannot find our way to God, who will forgive us and set us free. God did not build the wall—we did! And we are the ones who must tear it down.

So, how do we tear down the wall that we have built between us and God? The only way is to be honest with ourselves and remove the element of deception. The word *honest* means "free from deception."[3] In other words, we need to stop deceiving ourselves. Only then can we tear down the wall and truly know and understand that we are forgiven and set free. First John 1:6 and 8 says,

> If we claim to have fellowship with him [God] yet walk in the darkness, we lie and do not live by the truth. . . . If we claim to be without sin, *we deceive ourselves* and the truth is not in us (emphasis added).

So let's be totally honest with ourselves as we learn from the following verses.

Isaiah 59:3–4 teaches,

> For your hands are stained with blood, your fingers with guilt. Your lips have spoken lies, and your tongue mutters wicked things. No one calls for justice; no one pleads his case with integrity. They rely on empty arguments and speak lies.

Read the above verse again and underline the following phrases:

- Your lips have spoken lies.
- Your tongue mutters wicked things.
- No one pleads his case with integrity.
- Empty arguments and speak lies.

Now read Isaiah 59:3–4 again. What do you think these verses mean?

_____

_____

_____

Do you think these verses apply to you?

_____

_____

_____

Have you done any of these things when you chew on your cud?

_____

_____

_____

As you begin to be honest with yourself, think about what lies you have spoken. What empty arguments are you relying on? What case did you not plead with integrity? Is there someone—maybe a family member or a friend—whom you are still angry with about the initial hurt and pain? Perhaps you are still angry with the person who was responsible for causing you pain. Or perhaps you are angry with someone else—maybe your mom, your dad, or a loved one—because he or she didn't protect you from harm. Or perhaps you are angry with a friend because he or she let you down.

No matter who or what caused the hurt and pain, you need to honestly search your heart. Who are you angry with? Remember, there will be no peace in your heart until you are ready to admit this element of deception to yourself, confess it to God, and repent of the anger you hold in your heart toward another.

Psalm 139:23–24 is a wonderful passage to memorize:

> Search me, O God, and know my heart; test me and know my anxious thoughts. See if there is *any offensive way in me,* and lead me in the way everlasting (emphasis added).

Is there someone you are angry with?

_____

_____

_____

Are there any others? Be honest, and list everyone with whom you are angry.

_____

_____

_____

They were surprised to find the big wad of cud locked tight within their own hearts!

Each person I have discipled who has honestly looked deep within his heart and willingly admitted the *offensive way* in himself was surprised to discover the element of deception within the big wad of cud. The element of deception offends God because it includes anger and bitterness, which is sin. Many times, anger is locked tight within a chamber deep in our hearts, yet we deceive ourselves and deny its very existence. Until we are honest with ourselves, unlock this anger and, like the sinful woman, place it at Jesus' feet, we will not feel forgiven and set free. In other words, we will be deprived of peace.

Let me explain what I mean. Remember the argument I talked about at the beginning of this chapter? When you replay the incident over in your mind, it is like you take your case—your case of cud-chewing—to court. However, you do not plead the case with integrity, as we read in Isaiah 59:3–4. This court is, as Pastor Jon Courson states:

> . . . not a legal court on earth, nor an eternal court in heaven . . . so what court? It is the court that takes place in your *own* mind. You build a case daily, you bring in new witnesses, you gather more evidence, you build this case against him, against her, against them. You build this case; it's in your mind . . . it grows bigger. You hold the court case over and over and over again [as you chew on the big wad of cud] and here's the kicker—every time you hold court in your mind, *you win!* The other guy *never* wins. *You always win!* You always conclusively conclude, I'm right, they're wrong.[4]

The sad part is that even though in your mind you won, you are still the one who is hurting! Your empty arguments offer you no justice, and your pleadings have no integrity. Your heart will never be set free by trying to deny your sins—even the sin of anger hidden in your heart that you think no one can see. Remember, God sees all. He knows!

Proverbs 20:27 states,

> The lamp of the LORD searches the spirit of a man; it searches out his inmost being.

God sees all that is within your heart. Your anger toward your mother, your father, your sister, your brother, your friend, or whomever will deprive you of peace. It will continue to deprive you until you give it all to Jesus, just like the sinful woman did.

The choice is yours!

This is true even if you were sinned against—even if someone did something to hurt you deeply, something that was out of your control. The important point to understand is that the anger locked and hidden deep within your heart is something that you *do* have control over. You have a choice! You can choose to give the anger to God so that you will know and understand that you are forgiven and set free, or you can choose to hold onto the anger and be deprived of peace. But I must warn you: If you choose to hold on to the anger, it will cause the vicious downward spiral of sin, sin, and more sin to spin again, which in turn will cause the cruddy consequence-spitting to begin again in your life. As a result, you will remain like a cow, chewing the cud, and like a camel, spitting on those around you. The choice is yours. Which do you want: To know that you are forgiven and set free, or to be deprived of peace?

Hopefully, you have chosen to be forgiven and set free. So let's look at how you can do this. Psalm 4:4–5 explains an important principle:

> In your anger do not sin; when you are on your beds, search your hearts and be silent. Offer right sacrifices and trust in the LORD.

Ephesians 4:26 repeats this concept when it teaches,

> "In your anger do not sin": Do not let the sun go down while you are still angry.

What do you think these verses mean?

_____

_____

_____

Have you allowed the sun to go down on your anger? Have you gone to bed while you were still angry?

_____

_____

_____

God's Word does not say that we cannot be angry. It says, "In your anger do not sin" (Ephesians 4:26). God created us to have emotions, but He knows that if we stay angry for a long time, it will hurt us and cause the cruddy consequences to appear in our lives. That's why God's Word warns us not to go to sleep while we are still angry. If we do, we will stuff the anger deep within our inmost being, deep within our hearts.

Remember the verse you learned in chapter 1?

> The words of a gossip are like choice morsels; they go down to a man's inmost parts.
>
> —Proverbs 18:8; 26:22

When we stuff the anger deep within our hearts—deep within our inmost beings—we sin in our anger, because we don't give the anger to God in the manner that He intended. Therefore, we must learn to deal with our anger correctly. We should not lock it up tight in hidden chambers deep within our hearts, where it will become infected and poisonous.

The good news is that God has made a way for us to know without a doubt that we are forgiven and set free from all of the cud and cruddy consequences. We discover the key in 2 Corinthians 10:5:

> And we take captive every thought to make it obedient to Christ.

Second Corinthians 10:5 holds the key!

It is time for us to take every thought captive and make it obedient to Christ: every thought—all the hurt, all the pain, and all the anger, including the element of deception, by being totally honest with ourselves. We are to take all of this captive and make it obedient to Christ.

One of the definitions of *captive* is "to capture one's mind."[5] It is as if we capture all of the hurtful thoughts in our minds one last time by honestly admitting to ourselves that those thoughts are there. Then we make them obedient to Christ as we confess them to Him. The word *obedient* means to be submissive to authority. So once we take the hurtful thoughts captive by admitting that they are there, we give them to Jesus by confessing them, as we learned in chapter 3. We place them at His feet, just like the sinful woman did, and leave them there forever! When we do this, we are being submissive and obedient to the authority of Christ, because God never intended for us to hold onto the hurt, pain, and anger.

What are you to take captive?

_____

_____

_____

Once taken captive, what are you to do with it?

_____

_____

_____

There was a woman who once said to me, "Giving my anger to the Lord is not tangible." What she was saying was that she could not touch or see the anger as she gave it to the Lord. It was just in her imagination, and therefore it seemed unreal. What she said to me was true. In fact, the definition of *tangible* is "able to be touched."[6] Something that is not tangible is unable to be touched. I think this is what most people struggle with when they are told they must take the hurt, pain, and anger captive and make it obedient to Jesus Christ.

In view of this, I want to teach you a tangible way to touch and see your anger as you make it obedi-ent to Jesus Christ, and then leave it with Him forever. It's time to search your heart and to trust in the Lord. It's time to spend some time alone with the Lord and write a letter. First, ask Him to reveal any hurt, pain, and anger (including any element of deception) stuffed and locked deep within your heart. Honestly pray the following verse:

Search me, O God!

> Search me, O God, and know my heart; test me and know
> my anxious thoughts. See if there *is any offensive way in me,*
> and lead me in the way everlasting.
> —Psalm 139:23–24, emphasis added

It is interesting to note that the word *offensive* in verse 24
can also be translated as *hurtful, wicked,* and *grievous.* Think
about this for a moment. As you have chewed on your hurt,
pain, and anger, have you allowed it to become so hurtful to
yourself that it has become not only offensive to God but also
wicked and grievous to Him? Ephesians 4:30–31 says,

> Do not grieve the Holy Spirit of God, with whom you
> were sealed for the day of redemption. Get rid of all bitter-
> ness, rage and anger.

If that doesn't convince you to let go of your anger, consider
this: according to Strong's concordance, one definition of the
Hebrew word for *offensive* is *idol.*[7] Is it possible that you have
allowed the big wad of cud of hurt, pain, and anger to become
an idol in your life? An *idol* is anything you put before God
or in place of God. God is a jealous God, and He does not
want to share His rightful place in your heart with anyone or
anything, including the big wad of cud. When you choose to
hold onto hurt, pain, and anger (including any element of
deception), it can become a disgusting idol you worship and
protect within your heart, because you are placing it first in
your life before God.

After you have prayed the above verse in Psalms, ask God
to unlock the hidden chambers of your heart to show you
if there is any element of deception and *any offensive way* in
you that has become an idol in your life. Next, begin to write
whatever He puts on your heart. Use the letter as a tangible
tool to unlock the anger that you have hidden deep within.

Address the letter to whomever God puts on your heart and begin to write whatever comes to your mind. This letter is between you and God only—no one else will ever see it. So do not hold back! You may need to write more than one letter. One time when I was teaching about this tangible tool at a retreat, a woman, her face glowing with joy and peace, came up to me after the quiet time and said, "I just wrote 26 pages, and I've been set free!"

Let me share an interesting, true story with you to show how easily we can deceive ourselves about the anger in our hearts because we don't want to let it go. When my daughter was about to begin her freshman year of high school, we moved to Bulgaria in Eastern Europe to become missionaries. My daughter was excited about the move. Six months later, however, I began to see some cruddy consequences in her life. Now, I knew that she didn't have a major deep heart hurt as a result of abuse or something tragic in her life, so I didn't know where these cruddy consequences were coming from. I encouraged her to pray and ask God what was going on deep within her heart, but there was no change. The cruddy consequences continued, and even began to get worse.

I realized that it was time to teach my daughter how to get her heart right with God. We spent a few hours together, and I taught her everything that you have now learned up to this point. I then instructed her to take a quiet time with the Lord and ask Him to search her heart. I told her to ask God if she was angry with someone and, if so, who it was.

I explained to her that she was more than likely angry with her dad or me. Many times, the hurt, pain, and anger we feel is directed at someone we love deeply. It's part of life. Regardless of whether it is intentional or unintentional, we will be hurt by those we love. And because the person we're angry with is someone we love deeply, we try to deceive ourselves into believing we are not angry with him or her. It gets confusing between the feelings of love and the anger.

I think my daughter thought I was crazy, but I encouraged her and told her that it was OK for her to be honest with herself. I told her to write whatever God put on her heart, as the letter was going to be between her and Him only. After she completed the letter, I asked her if God had shown her anything. Was there someone with whom she had been angry? She smiled and said yes. I giggled and asked her if I was the one she had been angry with. Again, she smiled and answered with a big *yes*. I then asked her if God had shown her why she was angry. Once again, she said yes. She said that the reason that had been revealed to her when she wrote the letter was so strange that it surprised her. It was something she would never have guessed. She said that she had been angry at me because I had *made* her move to Bulgaria! Isn't that amazing? She had wanted to move to Bulgaria. She had been excited about this grand adventure. Yet months later, she was angry about it. Why?

While we were living in Bulgaria, our youth pastor back in California encouraged the youth group to send e-mails to the Fresonke girls to encourage them while they were on the mission field. Unfortunately, most of the e-mails included stories from the group about all of the activities that had been going on, such as trips to Disneyland and to the beach. Life in Bulgaria isn't that exciting, and soon my daughter was feeling that life was passing her by. As she continued to think about these things and chew on them, they became cud. Remember how the *cud* changes form? Soon her cud-chewing went from being excited about living in Bulgaria to feeling that I had *made* her move to this forsaken country. And as she held court in her mind, she even changed the facts!

Do you see how even the smallest hurt can turn into something big if it is not handled in the manner that God intended? If we don't bring our hurt and pain to Him, we soon find ourselves caught in the vicious downward spiral of sin, sin, and more sin. And we don't even realize it is happening, because of the element of deception.

This is why I want to encourage you to have a quiet time with the Lord. Ask Him to search your heart and to see if there is *any offensive way* in you—any element of deception deep inside. As you do this, do not hold anything back—including tears! If you begin to cry, let the tears flow, because it means that God is washing your heart. If you stop the tears, you will stop what God is softly trying to say to you.

Lead me in the way everlasting!

I want to stress that this *letter is never to be mailed.* If you were to mail it, in most cases it would only cause more hurt and pain and give you a whole new reason to chew the cud. This letter *is between you and God only* and is just a tool to allow you to see if there is hidden hurt or pain inside of you that you are unaware of—to see if there are any elements of deception or *any offensive way* locked deep within your heart.

After you write the letter, the next step is to offer right sacrifices and trust in the Lord *by letting go of the anger and giving it to God.* Remember what Psalm 4:4–5 says:

> In your anger do not sin; when you are on your beds, *search your hearts* and be silent. *Offer right sacrifices* and trust in the LORD (emphasis added).

According to God's Word, you are not to let the sun go down while you are still angry, and you are to offer right sacrifices and trust in the Lord.

You can do this in a very practical way by destroying the letter as you offer the anger to God as a right sacrifice. One of my favorite ways to do this is by burning the letter in a fireplace. A dear friend of mine once shared that after she burnt her letter, she felt the Lord impress on her heart,

> It is a burnt offering, an offering made by fire, an aroma pleasing to the LORD.
>
> —Leviticus 1:13b

If there is no fireplace available, tear the letter into tiny little pieces. If you are feeling really creative, you can even put some of the little pieces into a helium balloon and offer the anger as a right sacrifice to God by letting go of the balloon and watching it rise to Him. Burning, tearing, or sending the letter up in a helium balloon is another visual and tangible way of giving the hurt, pain, and anger, along with the element of deception or *any offensive way*, to God once and for all.

After many years of discipling people, I have seen that those brave enough to be honest with themselves and take a step of faith by writing the letter and giving the anger to God come to a place in which they truly know and understand deep within their hearts that they are forgiven and set free. Those who choose not to write the letters, or who do not choose to give the anger to God, stay in the vicious downward spiral of sin, sin, and more sin. Their lives continue to be filled with cruddy consequences.

The choice is yours! Which will it be?

The choice is yours! Which will it be: forgiven and set free, or afflicted with cruddy consequences for years to come?

The truth of what you have just learned is so freeing to me that I continue to do it whenever needed. When I realize that I am chewing on something not pleasing to God, I write out a letter to help me discover what is really taking place deep within my heart. I want to encourage you to take every thought captive and make it obedient to Christ. The moment that you do, "you will know the truth, and the truth will set you free" (John 8:32). What are you waiting for? Do it! Let it go so that you may *go in peace!*

DIGGING DEEPER

Spend some quiet time with God and write the letter(s) of anger as a visual and tangible tool to see what you have stuffed and hidden deep within your heart. Then offer the anger to Him so that you will finally know without a doubt that you are forgiven and set free. Burn, tear, or send the pieces of the letter up in a helium balloon. Do not hold onto it any longer. Let it go—once and for all. Next, take time to look up the following verses that prove the truth that you learned in this chapter. Underline or highlight them in your Bible. Then write them in a journal or on a 3×5 card so that you will have them close at hand when you need encouragement.

You are to take every thought captive—
  2 Corinthians 10:3–5
You are not to let the sun go down while you are still
  angry—Ephesians 4:26
You are to offer right sacrifices and trust in the Lord—
  Psalm 4:4–5
You are forgiven—Luke 7:48 and 50; 1 John 2:12
You are set free—Psalm 119:32; John 8:31–32;
  Galatians 5:13

CHAPTER FIVE

FORGIVENESS IS NOT AN OPTION

Now that we have learned how to be forgiven and set free, it is time to discover another important aspect to our Christian walk. In the previous chapter, we discussed how to give our anger to God. But, if you remember, when we choose to chew on the cud of hurt and pain, it changes form into the big wad of cud. This big wad of cud not only includes anger but also *bitterness*. It is now time to learn about this bitterness, because chewed up within the bitterness is a bitter poison known as unforgiveness.

The big wad of cud of hurt, pain, anger, and *bitterness*!

Lamentations 3:19–20 warns about this bitterness:

I remember my affliction and my wandering, the bitterness and the gall. I well remember them, and my soul is downcast within me.

In the original Hebrew, the word *bitterness* in this verse comes from the word *wormwood*, which was a bitter herb that the Hebrew people considered poisonous.[1] As you may recall, if we continue to chew the cud, it will turn into an infection that can poison our whole life. It is also interesting to note that in the original Greek of the New Testament, the word *bitterness* can mean extreme wickedness, a bitter root which produces a bitter fruit, and even bitter hatred.[2] This is why I believe God's Word warns us to make sure there is no root among us that produces such bitter poison.[3]

The only way for us to get rid of this unforgiveness, chewed up together with bitterness in the big wad of cud, is to learn how to forgive others. In the Greek, the word *forgive* can be translated as "to let go, to give up, [and] to keep no longer."[4] In other words, it's time for us to not only let go of the hurt and the anger we learned about in the last chapter, but also to give up the bitterness and unforgiveness. It's time to keep these things no longer and move on with our lives.

In the previous chapter, we learned how to give part of the big wad of cud to God—the part that includes the anger. Now, it is time for us to let go of every aspect of the wrong that has been done to us, so that we can give the other part of the big wad of cud to God—the part that includes the bitterness and unforgiveness. It is time for us to forgive so that we can be set free

Don't be captive to sin! Let go, give up and keep no longer!

from the bitterness, because if we do not, we will just begin to chew the cud again.

If this happens, the vicious downward spiral of sin, sin, and more sin will start anew, bringing with it all the cruddy consequences. Listen to what God's Word warns in Acts 8:23:

> For I see that you are full of bitterness and captive to sin.

If you and I are full of bitterness, which includes unforgiveness, we will be captive to the vicious downward spiral of sin, sin, and more sin. Soon, we will be right back where we were at the beginning of this book. That is not where we want to be!

Ephesians 4:31a clearly states what we need to do:

> Get rid of all bitterness, rage and anger.

What are we to get rid of?

_____

_____

_____

Are you ready to get rid of it?

_____

_____

_____

In view of this truth, let's discuss what Jesus taught about *forgiveness,* because He wants us to become victorious in this area of our lives. He wants us to be set free from all the cud-chewing and consequence-spitting and be more than

conquerors over this issue of bitterness and unforgiveness.
And He wants us to be at peace with God!

In Matthew 6:15, Jesus prayed,

> But if you do not forgive men their sins, your Father will
> not forgive your sins.

Jesus' prayer warns that if you and I are unwilling to forgive
others, our own hearts are in no condition to ask God the
Father to forgive us.[5] Think about it: If we are unwilling to
forgive others, what right do we have to ask God to forgive
our sins? God knows that unforgiveness will destroy you and
me. He knows that unforgiveness in our hearts will cause us
to continue to chew the cud. That is why forgiveness is not an
option. That is why, as we learned in the last chapter, it is time
for us to let go of not only the anger, but also the bitterness.

For this reason, it might be a good idea to look at what
forgiveness is and what forgiveness is not, so that we can
completely forgive the person who hurt us.[6] Let's first look at
what forgiveness is.

Forgiveness Is Modeled After God's Forgiveness of Us.

Because God has forgiven you and me, we need to forgive
others. In other words, we are called to be imitators of God.
Ephesians 4:32–5:1 admonishes,

> Be kind to one another, tenderhearted, forgiving one an-
> other, as God in Christ forgave you. Therefore be imitators
> of God, as beloved children.
>
> —ESV

Forgiveness Is a Step of Obedience.

We are to take every thought captive—even thoughts of unforgiveness—and make them obedient to Christ. Otherwise,

we are living in disobedience to God. Second Corinthians 10:5b teaches this important principle:

> We take captive every thought to make it obedient to Christ.

Forgiveness Is Leaving the Revenge to God.

If we make plans to get even with someone, we are only letting that person continue to hurt us. It is similar to what Proverbs 26:27 warns:

> Whoever digs a pit will fall into it, and a stone will come back on him who starts it rolling.
>
> —ESV

And Romans 12:19 warns,

> Do not take revenge, my friends, but leave room for God's wrath, for it is written: "It is mine to avenge; I will repay," says the Lord.

Forgiveness Is Expensive.

In Matthew 18:21–22, Peter came up to Jesus and asked Him,

> "Lord, how often shall my brother sin against me, and I forgive him? Up to seven times?" Jesus replied, "I do not say to you, up to seven times, but up to seventy times seven."
>
> —NKJV

According to Jewish teaching, a person was to forgive an offender four times. Peter, though more generous with his willingness to forgive up to seven times, was still setting a limit beyond which he did not need to forgive. When Jesus said "seventy times seven," He was telling Peter that he should forgive without limit.[7]

Forgiveness Is a Heart Issue.

Forgiveness is a heart issue!

Jesus said,

> Pay attention to yourselves! If your brother sins, rebuke him, and if he repents, forgive him, and if he sins against you seven times in the day, and turns to you seven times, saying, "I repent," you must forgive him.
> —Luke 17:3–4 ESV

You may have heard it said that you do not need to forgive someone if he or she does not repent—in other words, if the offender does not come to say that he or she is sorry. However, it is important to realize that just because the verse says *if he repents, forgive him*, it does *not* say that if the person doesn't repent, we don't forgive him or her. We cannot add what we like to God's Word. What this verse means is that forgiveness is a *heart issue*. We must have a heart that is always ready to forgive.

Psalm 86:5a says,

> For You, Lord, are good, and *ready* to forgive.
> —NKJV, emphasis added

If we are to model our forgiveness after God's forgiveness of us, we must also be ready to forgive. In other words, we cannot hold a grudge against a person just because he or she has not repented or asked for our forgiveness. If we are holding onto grudges and unforgiveness, the truth is not in us. We are just living by excuses and blaming others for our unwillingness to forgive. In other words, we are living in sin.

We need to remember that before we repented and asked God to forgive us for our sins, He still loved us and was waiting to say, "You are forgiven!" He was *ready* to forgive the moment we repented. We must therefore have hearts that have already done the deep work of forgiveness by letting go of the hurt and are *prepared* and *ready* to say, "I forgive you." It is only then that we will have no unforgiveness in our hearts, because we have already let it go and given it to God. In Mark 11:25, Jesus explained it this way:

> And when you stand praying, if you hold anything against anyone, forgive him.

Forgiveness Is a Promise.

In his book *From Forgiven to Forgiving,* Jay Adams states, "When our God forgives us, He promises that He will not remember our sins against us anymore. That is wonderful!"[8] When we are forgiven, God treats us as if we had never sinned. Again, if we model our forgiveness after God's forgiveness, we will also promise to treat the person who has wronged us as if he or she had never hurt us. Proverbs 19:11 shares a proverb to live by:

> A man's wisdom gives him patience; it is to his glory to overlook an offense.

Forgiveness Is for Our Own Sake.

We need to forgive the offender for our own sake. Ignoring this fact will cause us to dwell in the pit of despair. Listen to what God said in Isaiah 43:25:

> I, even I, am he who blots out your transgressions, for *my own sake,* and remembers your sins no more (emphasis added).

If God blots out our sins for His own sake, then this must be best for us as well. Forgiveness may or may not change the other person, but it will change us!

So let's recap what forgiveness is. Forgiveness is:

- Modeled after God's forgiveness of us
- A step of obedience
- Leaving the revenge to God
- Expensive!
- A heart issue
- A promise
- For our own sake

Forgiveness is . . .

From the list above, do you understand the seven things that forgiveness is?

_____

_____

_____

If not, which do you not understand?

_____

_____

_____

Note: If you do not understand what *Forgiveness is* turn to page 208 (appendix 2 titled "Answers to Questions") to learn more.

Now that we have looked at what forgiveness is, let's look at what forgiveness *is not*. It is important for us to know this distinction, because sometimes we can get feelings and emotions all wrapped up and confused when dealing with this issue. Remember, we are not to live by feelings, but by the truth of God's Word.

Forgiveness Is Not a Feeling.

Forgiveness is not something you or I *feel* like doing, but rather a step of obedience to Christ. As Jay Adams states, "Unlike modern discussions of forgiveness, there is nothing in the Bible about 'feelings of forgiveness' or 'having forgiving feelings' towards another."[9]

During World War II, Corrie ten Boom and her family hid Jews in their home. When they were discovered, they were arrested and put in a German concentration camp, where many of Corrie's family died. After World War II, God used Corrie to share His love with many who were hurt during the war. One of her main messages was about forgiveness.

After one particular meeting, an SS officer from the camp where Corrie and her sister Betsie had lived came up to Corrie and said, "Isn't it wonderful! Jesus has washed away my sins." He then reached out his hand and asked Corrie for forgiveness. Corrie did not have it in her heart to forgive. She did not *feel* like forgiving. In fact, she felt just the opposite. But she was obedient and asked God to give her the strength to forgive the man. "I can do all things through Christ who strengthens me" (Philippians 4:13, NKJV).

Corrie later stated that though she prayed for strength, her right hand remained limp by her side. She just couldn't bring herself to shake the hand of the man who had once stood by mocking, while she and her sister were forced to strip off their clothes and enter the shower room. "I can't do it, Lord," she said. "Don't ask me for this; it's too much." Her thoughts were angry and hurtful, yet she realized that she herself had demanded such an action from others who had suffered during the war. "Forgive your enemies," she had told them.

"Then help me, Lord," Corrie prayed. "I can't do it on my own." As she prayed, she suddenly felt power rush along her arm and generate warmth and forgiveness for the man who stood before her. Even now, he was eagerly shaking her hand. God had answered her prayer and provided.[10] Even though Corrie did not *feel* like forgiving the SS guard, she took the step of obedience, and God was faithful.

If you and I wait until we *feel* like forgiving, it will never happen. We will again begin to chew on the cud of all the hurt and pain until it grows into a big wad of anger, bitterness, and unforgiveness. If we continue to hold on to it, we will soon be spitting the cruddy consequences on all those around us whom we love. We will be caught up in the vicious downward spiral of sin, sin, and more sin, and our lives will again be captive to sin and out of control.

Do we really want that to happen? Remember, forgiveness is not a feeling. For this reason, we need to ask God to give us the strength to forgive, just like Corrie did. When we do, we will discover that we truly are strong in the Lord and more than conquerors. First Corinthians 13:4–5 explains it this way:

> Love is patient, love is kind. . . . it keeps no record of
> wrongs.

Forgiveness Is Not Holding onto Grudges.

The word *grudge* means "a feeling of deep-seated resentment
or ill will."[11] In Hebrew, the word *grudge* means "to keep."[12]
However, as we discussed at the beginning of this chapter, the
word *forgive* in the Greek of the New Testament can actually
be translated "to let go, to give up, [and] to keep no longer"—
which is the exact opposite of keep. We just discussed how
forgiveness is not a feeling. It is time to let go of any and all
wrong feelings associated with our deep heart hurts. It is time
to let go of any and all grudges that we may be hanging on to.
Leviticus 19:18 says it clearly:

> Never seek revenge or bear a grudge against anyone, but
> love your neighbor as yourself. I am the LORD.
>
> —NLT

Forgiveness Is Not Necessarily Understanding Why We Were Hurt.

In *Forgive and Forget,* Lewis B. Smedes notes, "We will probably never understand why we were hurt. . . . Understanding
may come later, in fragments, an insight here and a glimpse
there, after forgiving. But we are asking too much if we want to
understand everything at the beginning."[13] In the Bible, a man
named Joseph suffered incredible betrayal and hurt at the hands
of his brothers. However, when he later reflected on all that he
had been through, he told his brothers,

> You intended to harm me, but God intended it for good
> to accomplish what is now being done, the saving of many
> lives.
>
> —Genesis 50:20

Forgiveness Is Not Accepting the Bad Behavior.

Forgiveness is sometimes confused with accepting a person's wrongful actions. However, there is a difference between accepting a *person* and accepting that person's *behavior*. Forgiveness is not an acceptance of destructive, bad behavior, but an acceptance of the person regardless of his or her behavior. We learn this example from God, who accepts us and loves *us* but He does not accept our *sinful behavior*. Even though we hate the person's bad behavior—the sin—we are still called to forgive the sinner. Ephesians 4:32 states,

> Be kind and compassionate to one another, forgiving each other, just as in Christ God forgave you.

Forgiveness Is Not Tolerating Something Unpleasant.

To *tolerate* means "to put up with something or somebody unpleasant."[14] We do not have to tolerate or put up with something wrong or unpleasant when we forgive a person for the hurt he or she has caused. For example, imagine there was a man who lived on your block who had sexually assaulted you. He was arrested and sent to jail. Years later, when you were an adult, he was released and moved back into the house on your block. You had, through Christ's love, forgiven him years before for the hurt he caused you. But now you notice him inviting a young teenager (about the age you were when the assault happened) into his house. You would never accept or tolerate that kind of behavior. The man should be held accountable for the wrong he does, and you would protect another from suffering the harm that you suffered.

In Luke 23:41a, one of the criminals who hung on a cross next to Jesus said,

We are punished justly, for we are getting what our deeds deserve.

The criminal realized that he deserved the punishment for his crime. It is good that there were people around who did not tolerate his criminal activity.

Forgiveness Is Not Forgetting.

You can choose to leave it behind or you can choose to let it destroy your life . . . the choice is yours!

Jay Adams states, "The Bible never commands 'forgive and forget.' This is one of those old, unbiblical statements by which people often try to guide their lives that is (sic) utterly incorrect. If you try to forget, you will fail. In fact, the harder you try the more difficult you will find forgetting."[15]

Some people get confused by passages in Isaiah and Jeremiah in which God states He promises to forgive our sins and remember them no more.[16] But "forgetting" is not the same as "remembering no more." Adams states, "Obviously, the omniscient [all-knowing] God who created and sustains the universe does not forget, but He can [choose to] 'not remember'. . . . To 'not remember' is simply a graphic way of saying, 'I will not bring up these matters to you or others in the future . . . I will never use these sins against you.'"[17] The apostle Paul wrote,

> But one thing I do: forgetting what lies behind and straining forward to what lies ahead, I press on toward the goal for the prize of the upward call of God in Christ Jesus.
> —Philippians 3:13b–14 ESV

Forgetting what lies behind does not mean that we will fully forget the hurt that another has caused us—especially if the hurt was horrendous, as in the case of rape or abuse. But we can *choose* to let it go and leave it behind. Then, we can move forward because we have not allowed that hurt to destroy our lives any longer. The choice is ours! God sets a wonderful example of this in Jeremiah 31:34b when He states,

> For I will forgive their wickedness and will remember their sins no more.

Forgiveness Is Not an Option.

God knows that unforgiveness will destroy us. This is why forgiveness is not an option. So what do we do? We do what God's Word commands us to do:

> Bear with each other and forgive whatever grievances you may have against one another. Forgive as the Lord forgave you.
>
> —Colossians 3:13

Now, let's recap what forgiveness is not. Forgiveness is not:

- A feeling
- Holding onto grudges
- Understanding why we were hurt
- Accepting the bad behavior
- Tolerating something unpleasant
- Forgetting!
- An option!

Forgiveness is not . . .

From the above list, do you understand the seven things that forgiveness is not?

If not, which do you not understand?

Note: If you do not understand what *forgiveness is not* turn to page 209 (appendix 2 titled "Answers to Questions") to learn more.

Because forgiveness is not an option, are you ready to let go of any bitterness and unforgiveness that you are holding once and for all? Do you want to get rid of this bitterness and unforgiveness completely?

Many of us desire to be rid of unforgiveness but have no idea how to go about it. For years, we have held on to our bitterness, which has now turned into the bitter poison of unforgiveness. Although we are tired of it, the unforgiveness is comfortable to us, much like an old security blanket. However, we can discover the key in how to let go of the unforgiveness in our lives by once again listening to what Jesus said:

> But I say to you who hear, love your enemies, do good to those who hate you, bless those who curse you, *pray for*

those who mistreat you. . . . Be merciful, just as your Father is merciful.

—Luke 6:27–28, 36 NASB, emphasis added

Remember, you and I need to model our lives after Christ's life. Praying for those whom we have bitterness and unforgiveness against is the key that will set us free. As we see from the life of Jesus, even as He was being crucified He prayed over and over again.

Praying is the key that will set you free!

Then Jesus said, "Father, forgive them, for they do not know what they do."

—Luke 23:34a NKJV

The tense of the verb *said* indicates that Jesus repeated this prayer. As the soldiers nailed Him to the cross, He prayed, "Father, forgive them." When they lifted the cross and placed it in a hole in the ground, He prayed, "Father, forgive them." As He hung on the cross between heaven and earth and heard religious people mocking Him, He repeatedly prayed, "Father, forgive them."[18] We, too, need to pray like Jesus prayed.

Pray for those who mistreat you!

If there is bitterness and unforgiveness in your heart, Satan will use this as a stronghold in your life. He will shoot fiery darts aimed at the poisonous infection of bitterness and unforgiveness. When this happens, use prayer as a weapon to extinguish the fiery darts. Every time you are reminded of the past hurt, instead of dwelling and chewing on all the thoughts and feelings associated with it, *pray.* Pray just as Jesus taught:

Pray for those who mistreat you.

—Luke 6:28 NASB

Or, as the *English Standard Version* puts it,

Pray for those who abuse you.

No matter how horrendous the hurt you suffered, God calls you to let it go so that you may *go in peace!* If the person who injured you is not saved, pray for his or her salvation. If the person is saved, pray for him or her to draw closer to God. Now, it is true that you will not *feel* like praying this prayer. You may feel like Jonah felt—he did not want God to spare the Ninevites. You, too, may not want those who have caused you pain to be forgiven. However, forgiving that person is a step of obedience, not a feeling.

I have learned over the years that every time I was reminded of a past hurt, the key was to pray for the person who hurt me. As I was obedient to pray for that person, forgiveness came. Soon, I came to a point where I realized that whenever I thought of the person who hurt me, I really was praying from my heart for his or her salvation or for that person to draw closer to God. When this happened, I knew that the forgiveness in my heart was complete.

Second Corinthians 10:4 teaches,

The weapons we fight with are not the weapons of the world. On the contrary, they have divine power to demolish strongholds.

Use prayer as a mighty weapon to demolish the stronghold of bitterness and unforgiveness in your life.

Before moving on to the next chapter, write a letter of forgiveness to the same person or persons to whom you wrote the letter(s) of anger. This time, the letter must be one of *forgiveness*, not anger. Even if all you can do is write, "So and so, I forgive you" that is OK. Remember, forgiveness is not an option. It is a step of obedience,

Forgiveness is a step of obedience!

not some big gushy feeling. It is all right if you don't *feel* like forgiving. Just do it! Just let it go! You can do all things through Christ who strengthens you, because you are strong in the Lord and more than a conqueror.

After you write the letter, *keep* it, because God wants you to keep your forgiveness. As you forgive others and live your life according to His Word, you will be at peace with God and be all that He intends you to be. Once you take this step of obedience and forgiveness, you will *go in peace!*

Digging Deeper

No more excuses—go and write the letter. You can do it, because you are strong in the Lord and more than a conqueror. Then take the time to look up the following verses that prove the truth you learned in this chapter. Underline or highlight these verses in your Bible, and then write them in a journal or on a 3×5 card so that you will have them close at hand when you need encouragement.

> You are called to forgive—Mark 11:25;
>   Ephesians 4:32–5:1; Colossians 3:13
> You are to pray for those who mistreat you—Luke 6:28
> You are strong in the Lord—Isaiah 40:29–31
> You are more than a conqueror—Romans 8:37
> You are at peace with God—Psalm 29:11; 85:8; 119:165;
>   Isaiah 54:10; Romans 5:1

Extra Credit:

Read the story of Joseph in Genesis 37 and 39–50. Joseph was a young man whose brothers hated him and sold him into slavery. Years later, after much hard work, Joseph was falsely accused of rape and sent to prison. There, it appeared that he was forgotten, but God had a greater plan. Years later, Joseph said,

> You intended to harm me, but God intended it for good.
> —Genesis 50:20a

Therefore, we know as a fact, from his own words, that Joseph forgave those who had wronged him.

CHAPTER SIX

SET APART

Do you desire purpose and meaning in your life? Do you desire lasting peace and contentment? Now that you have learned how to give your deep heart hurts to God and be set free from all the cruddy consequences, it is time to learn about who you are, so that you can be all that God intends you to be. Then you can have a life filled not only with purpose and meaning, but also lasting peace and contentment. You are special to God, and you have been set apart for a specific purpose!

Recently, I read an interesting account of Queen Victoria's life. She was England's longest ruling monarch. She became queen when she was only 18 years old and ruled for 64 years. As the account I read stated:

> When she was young, Victoria was shielded from the fact that she would be the next ruling monarch of England lest this knowledge spoil her. When her teacher finally did let

her discover for herself that she would one day be Queen of England, Victoria's response was, "Then I will be good!" Her life would be controlled by her position. No matter where she was, Victoria was governed by the fact that she sat on the throne of England.[1]

From the moment Queen Victoria discovered the truth of who she was, she determined in her heart and mind to be good. She determined to walk worthy of her calling.

Well, much like Queen Victoria's teacher, I would like to help you discover who you are—who you are in Christ. For you, too, are royalty. You are a child of the King of kings. For this reason, you are sanctified. *Sanctified* means

You, too, are royalty!

to be "set apart"[2] and "to be free from sin."[3] There are two aspects to sanctification—a positional aspect and a practical aspect. The *positional aspect* has to do with the moment of your salvation. When you decide to give your heart to God and follow Him, you have immediately been set apart. The *practical aspect* has to do with how you live out your salvation. Each day, you must choose to make wise choices to be free from sin. Therefore, sanctification is both a *one-time event* and an *ongoing process* throughout your life.

We see these two aspects in Queen Victoria's life. Because of her royal birth, she knew that she would one day be the future queen of England. This was the positional aspect of her monarchy—the moment she was born, she was immediately in line to rule the country. However, the practical aspect of her rule occurred when she learned that she would one day be queen and made the declaration, "Then I will be good!"

From the moment she learned who she was and determined in her heart and in her mind to be good—to be the person that her birth and her position called her to be—she began the ongoing process of conducting her life in the way a queen should. In fact, on June 20, 1837, the day that Victoria was told that King William IV had died and she was now Queen of England, she wrote in her journal, "Since it has pleased Providence [God] to place me in this station, I shall do my utmost to fulfill my duty towards my country."[4]

I pray that you will also desire to fulfill your duty to be all that God intends you to be. If you do, you will have a life filled with purpose and meaning and have lasting peace and contentment. In this chapter, we will look at who you are in Christ *positionally* and also learn about the special privileges that are yours because of who you are in Christ.

You are loved by God, created in Christ Jesus, and complete in Him. You are not a mistake, for you are His workmanship, created in His image. You are His beloved. The moment you become born again and accept Christ as your Lord and Savior, you become a citizen of the kingdom of God. You become His child, chosen by Him, and are forever protected by Him. You are forgiven, redeemed, justified, and washed clean from your sins. You are a partaker of His divine nature. You are His and are always in His thoughts.

Now, because of this truth of who you are in Christ, God desires to have a real, personal, and intimate relationship with you. The word *intimate* means familiar, close, dear, personal, confidential, private, trusted, secret, deep, and detailed. These words describe the type of relationship that God truly desires to have with you—yes, you! He wants to be your friend, your confidant, your advocate, your supporter, your provider, your sympathizer, and your companion. These are other words that can be used to describe *intimate*. God desires to be your all-in-all, your best friend—the lover of your soul.

You have a choice!

Now, because of the deep love He has for you, He has given you a choice: You can choose to dwell within the Holy of Holies at the foot of His throne and learn how to be all that He intends you to be, or you can choose to settle for second or even third best. Let me explain about the Holy of Holies in which you are invited to dwell.

It has always been God's desire to dwell among His people. Yet ever since the Garden of Eden when Adam and Eve chose to sin, mankind has wandered from God's presence. Then, at Mount Sinai, God returned His presence and reestablished the long-lost relationship with His people.

It was at this time that God spoke to Moses and said,

> Then have them make a sanctuary for me, and I will dwell among them.
>
> —Exodus 25:8

This was to be a place where God's chosen people could come to hear from Him. It was a place where they could receive His love, forgiveness, and guidance. And so they made the Tabernacle. It is important to have a basic understanding of the pattern of this Tabernacle, because found within it was the Holy of Holies, and the clue to unlocking the secret of how to have a deep, personal, and intimate relationship with God.

God loves you so much that He wants to speak to you. Exodus 33:11a tells us that

The LORD would speak to Moses face to face, as a man speaks with his friend.

Psalm 84:2 shows how the psalmist yearned to meet with God:

My soul yearns, even faints, for the courts of the LORD; my heart and my flesh cry out for the living God.

Have you ever spent one day—or even one moment—in the presence of God? If you have, then your soul will yearn to be there again. What is more amazing is that you can spend every day in the Holy of Holies with God.

Many times when you are studying God's Word, you will see that God speaks to His people with pictures and parables (which is a biblical name for stories) so that they can picture the spiritual lesson He desires to teach. The Tabernacle is a visual picture of the intimate relationship that God desires to have with you. This visual picture can show you where your heart is spiritually concerning your relationship with God.

In her study "Dwelling in the Holy of Holies," Kay Smith states that there are three types of Christians in regard to where they live spiritually. We can draw this picture of the three types of Christians by relating them to the Tabernacle.[5] Basically, the Tabernacle had three parts: (1) the outer court, (2) the Holy Place, and (3) the Holy of Holies. The Holy of Holies was the place where God dwelt.

What three parts did the Tabernacle have?

_____

_____

_____

THE TABERNACLE
Exodus 25:8

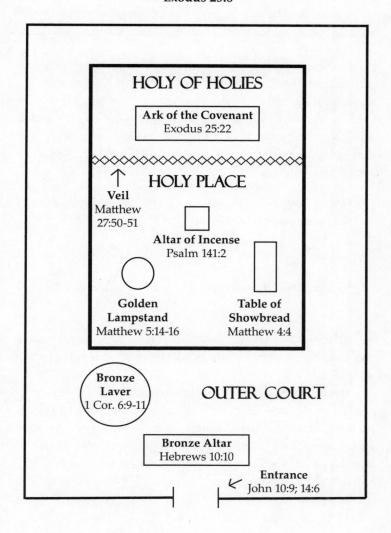

HOLY OF HOLIES

Ark of the Covenant
Exodus 25:22

HOLY PLACE

↑
Veil
Matthew
27:50-51

Altar of Incense
Psalm 141:2

**Golden
Lampstand**
Matthew 5:14-16

**Table of
Showbread**
Matthew 4:4

**Bronze
Laver**
1 Cor. 6:9-11

OUTER COURT

Bronze Altar
Hebrews 10:10

Entrance
John 10:9; 14:6

Where did God dwell?

_____

_____

_____

There was only one entrance to the Tabernacle, and that was through the door that led into the *outer court*. Now, remember, the Tabernacle can be a visual picture of our relationship with God. In the same way that there was only one way to God in the Tabernacle, there is only one way to God in our lives, and that is by accepting Jesus Christ as our Lord and Savior. In John 14:6, Jesus said,

> I am the way and the truth and the life. No one comes to the Father except through me.

He also said,

> I am the door. If anyone enters by me, he will be saved.
> —John 10:9a ESV

So the moment that you accepted Jesus Christ as your Lord and Savior, you entered the outer court in your relationship with Him.

Unfortunately, many Christians remain in the outer court and never go any deeper. They never enter into the deep, personal, intimate relationship that God desires to have with them. They have experienced the positional aspect of salvation, but they are not living out their Christian life on a practical day-by-day basis. They are not being all that God intends them to be.

Let's explore this by taking a look at the two items found within the outer court: the Bronze Altar and the Bronze Laver.

The *Bronze Altar*, also known as the Altar of Sacrifice, was a large piece of furniture that was used to make sacrifices in Old Testament days before Jesus came.[6] As John Schmitt and Carl Laney explain, "The position of the altar near the entrance of the Tabernacle reminds us of our need for atonement [our need to have our sins paid for by Christ's death] as the basis for approaching a holy God. The altar serves as a visual lesson, anticipating the perfect sacrifice that Christ offered on the cross."[7]

Once Christ died on the cross, there was no longer any need to offer sacrifices for man's sin. The sacrifice was made once, for all. Hebrews 10:10 teaches about this sacrifice that Jesus made so that we can enter into the outer court:

> And by that will we have been sanctified through the offering of the body of Jesus Christ once for all.
>
> —ESV

The *Bronze Laver* was the second item in the outer court. It was filled with water and was used for ceremonial washings. The Bronze Laver illustrates our need for spiritual cleansing from sin.[8] Remember, we are all sinners. First Corinthians 6:9–11 explains clearly what would happen to each of us if we were not washed by the blood of Jesus Christ:

> Do you not know that the wicked will not inherit the kingdom of God? Do not be deceived: Neither the sexually immoral nor idolaters nor adulterers nor male prostitutes nor homosexual offenders nor thieves nor the greedy nor drunkards nor slanderers nor swindlers will inherit the kingdom of God. And that is what some of you were. *But you were washed, you were sanctified, you were justified in the name of the Lord Jesus Christ and by the Spirit of our God* (emphasis added).

Keeping these two objects in mind, let's go back to our picture of the Tabernacle and where each type of Christian is spiritually in his or her relationship with God. *Outer Court Christians* are those who have received salvation but have gone no further in their relationship with God. They have received the sacrifice that Jesus Christ made on the cross when He died for their sins (as the Bronze Altar represents) and have been washed clean (as the Bronze Laver represents), but that's it. It's as if they entered through the door to the outer court when they accepted Jesus Christ and just stopped there. They have experienced the *positional aspect* of salvation, but are not practically living out their salvation in the manner God intended.

These Christians are not becoming all God desires them to be. They are missing out. They have no witness for God and continue to live their lives by their feelings and their fleshly desires. They will never find purpose, meaning, or lasting peace and contentment by remaining in the outer court. They are right where Satan wants them to be.

Remember, there is a battle going on that we cannot see—a battle that includes you and me. Satan does not want us to draw near to God and become all that He desires us to be. Satan wants to keep us ineffective so that we will not be a light and impact others for Christ. In view of his schemes, it is important to know that God does not want us to live our lives in the outer court. He has so much more for us. He wants a personal and intimate relationship with you and me.

Describe Outer Court Christians. Are they saved? Have they accepted Jesus Christ as their Savior?

_____

_____

_____

Are they becoming all who God wants them to be?

_____

_____

_____

Does the Outer Court Christian's life have purpose and meaning or lasting peace and contentment?

_____

_____

_____

Do you desire to be an Outer Court Christian? Or do you want more in your relationship with God? Why?

_____

_____

_____

Now, let's return to our picture of the Tabernacle. Beyond the outer court was the *Holy Place*. There were three items of furniture in the Holy Place that apply to our lives: (1) the Table of Showbread, (2) the Altar of Incense, and (3) the Golden Lampstand.

The purpose of the *Table of Showbread* was to display 12 loaves of bread as a continual thank offering to God for His many blessings. Here again is another spiritual lesson.[9] In Matthew 4:4, Jesus said,

> It is written: "Man does not live on bread alone, but on every word that comes from the mouth of God."

This is why the Bible is referred to as "the Bread of Life." It is important to read the Bible daily. We cannot survive on just physical food. We need spiritual food as well.

The *Altar of Incense*, as the name implies, was the place in which the priests burned incense as an offering to the Lord. In Scripture, incense often symbolizes prayer.[10] Psalm 141:2 teaches,

> May my prayer be set before you like incense; may the lifting up of my hands be like the evening sacrifice.

Prayer is the way in which we talk to God.

The oil lamps in the *Golden Lampstand* provided light to the priests who ministered within the darkened interior of the Holy Place. Matthew 5:14–16 explains how this applies to the Christian's life.[11] Jesus said,

> You are the light of the world. A city on a hill cannot be hidden. Neither do people light a lamp and put it under a bowl. Instead they put it on its stand, and it gives light to everyone in the house. In the same way, let your light shine before men, that they may see your good deeds and praise your Father in heaven.

As we read God's Word each day and pray, we begin to become a light unto the Lord. Others begin to see Christ in us.

Let's go back to our visual of the three types of Christian. Unlike the Outer Court Christian, the *Holy Place Christian* enters into the Holy Place by spending time in prayer and reading God's Word. Thus, his or her life begins to become a light unto God. But this Christian is still missing the most important aspect of his or her relationship with God: *intimacy*. Because of this, the Holy Place Christian still lives by his or her feelings and desires, which causes no purpose, meaning, or lasting peace and contentment in his or her life.

Contentment means "happiness with one's situation in life."[12] In other words, it means being fulfilled and satisfied regardless of what is happening. Holy Place Christians are not truly fulfilled and satisfied. They are not content. They spend some time with the Lord, which is a good thing, but then go about their day in their own strength. They try to find peace and contentment in things and situations, instead of in God. They are still living their lives by feelings and fleshly desires. They are not living by the truth of God's Word or seeking Him for His love, forgiveness, and guidance. As Kay Smith notes, "They will give the Lord an hour or two, but that's it. They want the rest of the time for self."[13] Elisabeth Elliot also explains, "By trying to grab fulfillment everywhere, [they] find it nowhere."[14]

Like the Outer Court Christian, the Holy Place Christian is also missing out. And you and I will be missing out as well if we remain in the Holy Place. We will *not* find true purpose and meaning or lasting peace and contentment in our lives if we remain in the Holy Place. God desires a deeper intimate relationship with us. In fact, He desires to be involved in every aspect of our lives. He wants to be our all-in-all.

Describe Holy Place Christians. Are Holy Place Christians living by the truth of God's Word or by their feelings and desires?

_____

_____

_____

What important aspect of their relationship with God is still missing?

_____

_____

_____

Because this intimacy with God is still missing, have Holy Place Christians found purpose and meaning or lasting peace and contentment in their lives?

_____

_____

_____

Do you desire to be a Holy Place Christian? Or do you want more in your relationship with God? Why or why not?

_____

_____

_____

This brings us to the *Holy of Holies.* This was the place where God dwelt. The high priest could only enter the Holy of Holies one day each year. That day was called Yom Kippur, the Day of Atonement. On this day, the high priest would go in and make atonement for the sins of the people.

Because the Holy of Holies was so holy, only the high priest could enter, and he had to go through a whole ritual to cleanse himself beforehand. If the priest wasn't cleansed or his heart wasn't right before God, God could zap him

God might zap him!

right on the spot. For this reason, the high priest wore bells on his robe so that the others could hear him walking around in the Holy of Holies and know that he was still alive. In addition, because no one else could enter, they tied a rope to his leg in case he got zapped so they could pull him out.

Now, pay attention to this next part—Satan would love for you to miss what you are about to learn. Separating the Holy Place from the Holy of Holies was the *veil*. This also has significance in our lives. The moment that Jesus Christ died on the cross for you and me, the veil was torn in two. Matthew 27:50–51 states it this way:

> And Jesus cried out again with a loud voice, and yielded up His spirit. Then, behold, the veil of the temple was torn in two from top to bottom.
>
> —NKJV

This is a visual picture that shows you and me that we are now able to enter into the Holy of Holies and meet with God personally. No matter what we have done or how bad we have been, God wants to meet with us! Listen to what Charles Spurgeon said back in the 1800s concerning the veil:

> Yet the rending [tearing] of the veil of the temple is not a miracle to be lightly passed over. It was made of "fine twined linen . . ." This gives the idea of a substantial fabric, a piece of lasting tapestry, which would have endured the severest strain. No human hands could have torn that sacred covering; and it could not have been divided in the midst by any accidental cause; yet, strange to say, on the instant when the holy person of Jesus was rent by death, the great veil which concealed the holiest of all [the Holy of Holies] was "rent in twain [torn in two] from the top to

the bottom." What did it mean? It meant much more than I can tell you now.[15]

This was a miracle—that's what it means! There was no way that the veil could have been torn by anyone other than God. When the veil was torn in two, it proved that God desires a deep, personal, and intimate relationship with you and me. We no longer have to go through some cleansing ritual like the high priest had to do to enter the presence of God. No matter where we have been or what we have done, we won't be zapped! God simply wants us to come and spend intimate time with Him in fellowship. He doesn't want us to be satisfied by only reading His Word and praying. He wants more.

When the veil was torn in two from top to bottom, what did this prove?

_____

_____

_____

Does God desire to have an intimate and personal relationship with you?

_____

_____

_____

God desires an intimate relationship with you and me. He loves us. He wants to be our all-in-all, our best friend, the lover of our souls. That is why He made a way for us to enter the Holy of Holies—so we can be near to Him.

There was one piece of furniture in the Holy of Holies, and that was the *Ark of the Covenant* (also known as the Ark of the Testimony). The Ark was a reminder to the Israelite people of God's personal presence. He desired to meet with them and speak to them.[16] In Exodus 25:22, God declared,

> There, above the cover between the two cherubim that are over the ark of the Testimony, *I will meet with you* (emphasis added).

Let's go back to our visual of the three types of Christians. Unlike the Outer Court Christian or even the Holy Place Christian, the *Holy of Holies Christian* desires to become all that God intends him or her to be. Holy of Holies Christians desire for God to be their all-in-all. They live by the truth of God's Word, not by their feelings and desires.

The Holy of Holies is not just a place but also an attitude of the heart. This is where our relationship with God moves from our heads to our hearts. It is here in the Holy of Holies that we realize who God is—He is amazing, the almighty God, the King of glory. He is all-powerful, all-knowing, and unchanging, yet He loves us and wants to be involved in every aspect of our lives.

It is in the Holy of Holies that we seek God daily, sometimes moment by moment, to receive His love, forgiveness, and guidance. It is here that He sees the yuck of our hearts and decides to love us anyway. It is here that we fall to our knees and offer our heart to Him to be changed. When we become Holy of Holies Christians, we realize that sin builds a wall between us and God and breaks our fellowship with Him. Therefore, we are continually aware of the sin in our own hearts and take immediate action to admit, confess, and repent of it so that our intimate relationship with God is restored. Psalm 139:23–24 becomes a way of life:

> Search me, O God, and know my heart; test me and know my anxious thoughts. See if there is any offensive way in me, and lead me in the way everlasting.

It is in the Holy of Holies that God takes our hearts and molds us into all He desires us to be when we come to Him in truth. It is here that we find our purpose and meaning for life. It is here that we discover lasting peace and contentment for every situation in life.

God wants to be involved in every aspect of our lives—in our living, breathing, waking, and sleeping; in our hurting, weeping, cleansing, and healing; in our laughing, hoping, dreaming, and waiting. He wants to be our best friend—the lover of our souls. It is only in the Holy of Holies that we can meet Him and grow to become all that He intends for us to be. It is here where we will learn how to practically live out who we are in Christ.

Describe the Holy of Holies Christian. Does the Holy of Holies Christian desire to be all that God intends him or her to be?

_____

_____

_____

Is the Holy of Holies Christian constantly aware that sin breaks intimacy with God?

_____

_____

_____

How is intimacy with God restored?

_____

_____

_____

Is the Holy of Holies Christian's life filled with purpose, meaning, lasting peace, and contentment?

_____

_____

_____

Where have you been dwelling? Put a checkmark next to the following description that would best describe your relationship with God.

Put a √ next to the
one that would
best describe your
relationship
with God

❑ *Outer Court Christian*—You are saved, but that's it! You have received the sacrifice that Jesus made on the cross for you. You are washed clean from your sins, but you are missing out on all that God has for you.

❑ *Holy Place Christian*—You spend time reading God's Word and praying. However, you are still missing the most important aspect of your relationship with God: intimacy. Because of this, there is no lasting contentment in your life. You continue to run after this or that to find satisfaction and pleasure. You don't look to God to be your all and all.

❏ *Holy of Holies Christian*—You desire to know God intimately. You realize that sin breaks fellowship with God, and because of this, you search your heart daily to make sure that there is no offensive way in you. You desire to be all that God intends for you to be. You have purpose, meaning, lasting peace, and contentment in your life.

Which are you?

_____

_____

_____

Is this where you desire to be?

_____

_____

_____

If not, what can you do to become a Holy of Holies Christian?

_____

_____

_____

In *Anna and the King,* one of my favorite movies, there is a scene that beautifully illustrates exactly the kind of relationship God desires to have with us. The movie is based on a true story about an English schoolteacher named Anna Leonowens.[17] In the movie, Anna has been hired to tutor the son of the King of Siam. Shortly after she arrives in Siam, she finds that she isn't being treated in the manner she was promised before she took the job. Her patience begins to wear thin, and she demands to meet with the king.

Each day, Anna goes to the court and waits to meet with the king to discuss this lack of manners. Each day, her hopes are dashed when court ends and she hasn't been allowed to speak to the king. So, one day she decides to take matters into her own hands. She approaches the king without permission—a stunt that almost costs Anna and her son their lives. The king's guards react immediately. They raise their swords to protect their king and strike them dead. Because of who she was positionally—an unknown English schoolteacher—she was unable to approach the king.

Yet, when Anna's son and the king's oldest son later get into a fight, the king's favorite daughter is so troubled that she takes off to find her daddy. The king is holding court, seated on his throne, taking care of all the important business for the country of Siam, when his precious little daughter runs in past all the guards, through their legs, past all the court officials and up the steps to her daddy. She jumps into his lap and whispers in his ear. He stops everything. He bends down to listen in love to her concern, and then he carries her away to go off to solve her problem.

The choice is yours!

This is a beautiful picture of how our relationship with the King of kings can be. He loves us. Because of who we are in Christ *positionally*, you and I have the right to enter into the King's presence. We are His children. No one will stop us as we enter into the Holy of Holies, because we have every right to be there. We will not be zapped. God loves us and, according to His Word, we are able to approach Him with confidence. But He gives us a choice: We can choose to

111

sit at His feet in the Holy of Holies and become all He wants us to be, or we can choose to live our lives by our feelings and fleshly desires, running after this or that but never being truly satisfied. The choice is ours.

God truly desires to have a deep, personal, intimate relationship with you. You have the privilege to come into His presence. In fact, because of who you are in Christ positionally, you not only have the privilege but also the right to draw near to Him. You are able to approach the King with confidence.

Satan will do everything in his power to keep you from becoming all that God intends for you to be. Satan is hoping that you will not become a Holy of Holies Christian. In view of this, take some time today to enter the Holy of Holies in your relationship with God. Spend some quiet time reading His Word and in prayer. But

Write whatever God puts on your heart!

don't stop there. Go deeper and enter into the Holy of Holies! Spend time just sitting at God's feet, meeting with Him and listening to His still, small voice. Ask Him to mold you and make you into the person He desires you to be. Ask Him to search your heart to see if there is any offensive way in you. Ask Him to lead you and to guide you.

Then take some blank paper or grab a journal and write whatever God puts on your heart. He wants to talk to you. Are you willing to listen? If you are, you will *go in peace!*

DIGGING DEEPER

Remember, the choice is yours. If you desire to fulfill God's purpose for your life, spend some quiet time today at His feet in the Holy of Holies. Open your Bible, pray and listen, and then write whatever He puts on your heart. He wants to speak with you.

In this chapter you learned many truths of who you are in Christ. Listed on the next page are those that you have not already learned about in the previous chapters. Take time to look up these verses and then underline or highlight them in your Bible. Next, write any that are special to you in a journal or on a 3×5 card so that you will have them close at hand when you need encouragement.

You are set apart—Leviticus 20:26; Psalm 4:3;
2 Timothy 2:21

You are royalty—1 Peter 2:9

You are sanctified—1 Corinthians 6:11;
1 Thessalonians 4:3–8

You are complete in Him—Colossians 2:10

You are His beloved—Colossians 3:12;
2 Thessalonians 2:13

You are a citizen of the kingdom of God—
Ephesians 2:19

You are chosen by Him—Ephesians 1:4;
1 Thessalonians 1:4

You are protected by Him—Joshua 1:5–9

You are redeemed—Galatians 3:13

You are justified—Romans 3:24 and 5:1

You are a partaker of His divine nature—2 Peter 1:4

You are the apple of His eye—Deuteronomy 32:10;
Psalm 17:8

You are His—Ezekiel 16:8

You are always in His thoughts—Psalm 139:17–18;
Isaiah 49:15–16

You are a light—Matthew 5:14–16; Ephesians 5:8

You are near to Jesus—Ephesians 2:13; James 4:8

You are able to approach the King with confidence—
Hebrews 10:19–22

Extra Credit:

Read about the Tabernacle in Exodus chapters 25–40.

CHAPTER SEVEN

WALK WORTHY

Now that we have looked at who we are in Christ *positionally*, it is time to discuss the spiritual battle that surrounds you and me that we cannot see. In this way, we will be prepared and equipped to *practically* live out who we are in Christ.

We are children of the King, and anytime the throne is involved, there will be warfare. Satan wants to trip us up. He wants to cause us to stumble and fall. He does not want us to walk worthy of our calling. Remember, he thinks up the lie, the world sells the lie, and, when we are not prepared and equipped for battle, our flesh buys the lie. In view of this, it is important to learn how to fight the good fight.

Each of us will struggle with the desires of our hearts. We will struggle with the thoughts of our minds. And we will struggle with the actions of our steps. But God has made a way for you and me to be victorious. He has made a way so that we are able to walk worthy of our calling. The battle belongs to Him. Psalm 24:8 declares this truth:

> Who is this King of glory? The LORD, strong and mighty, the LORD, mighty in battle!
>
> —ESV

She determined to walk worthy of her calling!

To set the stage for this chapter, let's go back to our story of Queen Victoria. Remember that when Victoria was young and discovered for the first time that she would one day be queen of England, her response was, "Then I will be good!"[1] The moment she discovered the truth of who she was, she determined to be the person whom her birth and position called her to be. In her heart and her mind, she determined to walk worthy of her calling in a *practical* manner. Her choice would greatly impact her life and the lives of everyone around her.

You and I also have a choice. We can make the wise choice to live up to our position in Christ by determining in our hearts and minds to walk worthy of our calling. Or we can make the foolish choice to live our lives by our feelings and desires. Let me explain.

Many make foolish choices based on feelings and desires!

Many times, we make choices based on our feelings and desires instead of on the truth of who we are in Christ. I have known many people who made some very foolish choices based on their feelings and desires—

including myself. For this reason, let me share a true story of someone who determined to walk worthy of her calling and make wise choices.

As I mentioned previously, when my daughters were in high school, we moved to Bulgaria as missionaries. Because one of my daughters has naturally blonde hair and blue eyes, she tends to stand out in this country. One day when a group of us were walking down a street in Sofia, Bulgaria, a young man suddenly came up, put out his arm all gentlemanly-like and charmingly said to her, "Ooh, baby, walk away with me!"

I can tell you that, at that moment, I felt like a momma bear ready to protect her young. I wanted to get in that young man's face and say, "Do you know who you are talking to? She is the daughter of the King, and you have no right to treat her so disrespectfully!" But it was unnecessary. My daughter didn't miss a step. She didn't bat an eye. She didn't even look his way. In fact, she ignored him completely and kept on walking. Why? Because she knew who she is in Christ! She knew that she is the daughter of the King. She knew that God loves her and has a plan for her life. She was not going to let some smooth-talking loser, who was not treating her worthy of her calling, turn her head and cause her to stumble and fall.

When my daughter was a young teen, she determined in her heart and her mind to walk worthy of her calling. She determined in her heart and her mind to fight the good fight. She determined in her heart and her mind to remain pure until marriage. Her reason? She didn't want to scar her heart for her husband. In other words, she knew that wrong relationships lead to deep heart hurts that can have lasting impact and consequences.

My daughter determined in her heart and her mind, just as Queen Victoria did, to walk worthy of her calling and not live her life by her feelings and desires. We all desire to be loved and accepted. These desires are normal. It is what we do with these desires that sets us apart. When we put our feelings and fleshly desires ahead of who we are in Christ, we will suffer the consequences.

When I was a teen, I didn't know the truth of who I was in Christ. I was an Outer Court Christian. I didn't even make it into the Holy Place by reading God's Word, let alone the Holy of Holies, where I could have found the strength and guidance I needed to be victorious. Instead, I lived by my feelings and desires. I followed the lies of Satan and the ways of the world, which led me to make some very foolish choices—choices that adversely impacted my life for many years.

It all began with my desire to feel loved and accepted. Satan played on my feelings and desires, and I believed his lies. Because of this, I had a wrong idea of love. I thought that if I had a boyfriend, I would feel loved and accepted. I never realized that by trying to find love in all the wrong places, I was only hurting myself and causing much of my deep heart hurt. This led to some pretty cruddy consequences in my life.

One foolish choice led to another foolish choice!

At 16, I found myself scared and alone. One foolish choice had led to another foolish choice, and my life was out of control. My desire to feel loved and accepted soon led me to the vicious downward spiral of sin, sin, and more sin—the downward spiral of wrong relationships, sexual immorality, pregnancy outside of marriage, abortion, alcohol, drugs, and suicidal thoughts, to name just a few. There seemed to be no way out.

I pray that you will determine in your heart and in your mind to walk worthy of your calling, just as Queen Victoria and my daughter did. I pray that you will *not* make the same foolish choices that I did. And I pray that even if you have made some foolish choices, you will realize it is not too late to change your ways and walk worthy of your calling. However, to do this, you will need to learn about the *practical aspect* of who you are in Christ.

You are able to fight the good fight. You are able to be victorious. You are able to walk worthy of your position in Christ. This is the reason for the battle. When you walk worthy in your calling, you are a light unto God. This is attractive to people, and Satan knows that people are watching you. He does not want others to see that something is different in your life and have them come to know Christ. He does not want their lives to be changed. He does not want them to become victorious. So he will do whatever he can to derail you and make you feel insecure in your calling.

Put on the whole armor of God!

However, God has made a way for you to live out the *practical aspect* of who you are in Christ. He has made a way for you to be fully equipped with the armor of God for the spiritual battle that you will face. Ephesians 6:10–18 teaches about this spiritual battle and the armor of God:

> Finally, my brethren, be strong in the Lord and in the power of His might. Put on the whole armor of God, that you may be able to

stand against the wiles of the devil. For we do not wrestle against flesh and blood, but against principalities, against powers, against the rulers of the darkness of this age, against spiritual hosts of wickedness in the heavenly places. Therefore take up the whole armor of God, that you may be able to withstand in the evil day, and having done all, to stand. Stand therefore, having girded your waist with truth, having put on the breastplate of righteousness, and having shod your feet with the preparation of the gospel of peace; above all, taking the shield of faith with which you will be able to quench all the fiery darts of the wicked one. And take the helmet of salvation, and the sword of the Spirit, which is the word of God; praying always with all prayer and supplication in the Spirit, being watchful to this end with all perseverance and supplication for all the saints.

—NKJV

The apostle Paul wrote these words while he was in prison. He realized that Christians are in the midst of a spiritual battle. God used Paul to give this word picture of the spiritual armor to tell Christians that they can fight the good fight, be victorious, and walk worthy of their calling. As you take up this spiritual armor, you will learn how to guard against all of Satan's schemes. You will learn how to be prepared and equipped for battle so that you can live out who you are in Christ *practically*. In view of this, let's take a look at each piece of this spiritual armor.

First, Paul tells you to gird your waist with truth. This piece of armor, also known as the *belt of truth,* represents the truth of the Word of God. Because you are called to guard your life, the belt of truth speaks of living your life in such a way that your actions and motives are governed by the Word of God.

This is why it is vitally important to read God's Word daily, so that you will be able to make wise and godly choices. The belt of truth must fully surround, encircle, and encompass every aspect of your life, just as a normal belt would. As God's Word fully encircles every aspect of your life and you begin to make wise choices, you will discover true victory in your life.

Let me give you an example of making wise choices based on God's Word. Let's say you desire to feel accepted. One of the ways to fit in and be accepted is to talk and cuss just like everyone else. However, you read in Ephesians 4:29,

> Don't use foul or abusive language. Let everything you say be good and helpful, so that your words will be an encouragement to those who hear them.
>
> —NLT

Because of this, you decide to follow God's Word and not swear. This is wearing the belt of truth! You allow God's Word to fully encircle this aspect of your life.

What does the belt of truth represent?

_____

_____

_____

What aspect of your life must the Word of God fully encircle?

_____

_____

_____

Do you have any examples from your life where you based a decision you made on God's Word?

_____

_____

_____

The *breastplate of righteousness* is the next essential piece of armor, as it guards your heart. Proverbs 4:23 warns,

> Above all else, guard your heart, for it affects everything you do.
>
> —NLT

Your heart enables you to have an intimate relationship with God and meet with Him in the Holy of Holies. As you meet with God, you move the truth of who you are in Christ from your head to your heart so that you can make wise choices. When you choose to believe in your heart, and make decisions based on the truth of who you are in Christ and not on your feelings and desires, you wear the breastplate of righteousness.

The story I told you about my daughter is a great example of someone wearing the breastplate of righteousness. Because she knew in her heart who she is in Christ, she was not going to let some smooth-talker turn her head and cause her to stumble and fall. The same is true for you. As you move the truth of who you are from your head to your heart and make wise choices based on this truth, you will be wearing your breastplate of righteousness!

What does the breastplate of righteousness guard?

_____

_____

_____

When do you have the breastplate of righteousness on? (This is very important to know, so take some time to search out the answer in the last two paragraphs.)

_____

_____

_____

Do you know that you are loved, forgiven, victorious, and able to walk worthy of your calling?

_____

_____

_____

Do you believe, in your heart, the truth of who you are in Christ?

_____

_____

_____

The next piece of armor is the *sandals of peace*. You are called to guard your actions because people are watching you. As you *shod your feet with the preparation of the gospel of peace*, you prepare the way for others to come to know Christ. In other words, as you walk worthy of your calling by making wise choices based on who you are in Christ, you are a light unto God and reflect His glory. Your actions speak louder than your words. People watch how you live, and sometimes your life will be the only Bible they will read. This is why you need to have your feet shod with the gospel of peace and live your life in such a way that people will want to come to know Christ.

In my own life, I have seen the importance of having my feet shod with the preparation of the gospel of peace. I have had my share of heartaches and trials. A few examples: my sister being diagnosed with a brain tumor, my niece's 20-month-old baby being burned over 35 percent of her body, family members getting sick and dying within a few months of each other, and my living with lupus daily—a very painful, life-threatening, chronic disease. However, as my family and I walked through the midst of these situations, it prepared the way for us to share the gospel of peace, and as a result, some came to know Christ! This is having your feet shod with the sandals of peace.

What do you prepare the way for as you shod your feet with the gospel of peace?

_____

_____

_____

What speaks louder than words?

_____

_____

_____

Another important piece of armor is the *shield of faith.* As you begin to live your life based on the truth of who you are in Christ, Satan will shoot his fiery darts at you in an attempt to destroy your faith and your relationship with God. Satan hopes that the fiery darts will hit their target, burst into flames, and start a wildfire that will be almost impossible to extinguish. Your shield of faith will give you the confidence to live your life based on the truth of who you are in Christ and equip you to resist Satan's attacks. Your faith in God and His Word will quench those fiery darts and give you the strength to walk worthy of your calling.

Hebrews 11:1 defines *faith* as "being sure of what we hope for and certain of what we do not see." Having faith means trusting in God and His promises.[2] Therefore, when you begin to worry about everything around you—just stop! As Isaiah 26:3a states,

> You will keep in perfect peace him whose mind is steadfast.

So instead of focusing on everything that is causing you to worry, pick up the shield of faith and stay focused on God and His promises. When you decide by faith to have your mind steadfast on Him and His promises, you are using the shield of faith effectively.

What quenches Satan's fiery darts?

_____

_____

_____

What does faith in God and His Word give to you?

_____

_____

_____

How do you use the shield of faith effectively?

_____

_____

_____

The next piece of armor is the *helmet of salvation*. As a Christian, you are called to protect your mind. Satan wants to destroy your thought life, and he will do this by playing on your feelings and desires in an attempt to hold your mind captive. Many times, your feelings will trigger your desires, your desires will trigger your thoughts, and your thoughts will trigger your actions. Therefore, if you do not protect your mind, you allow Satan to influence you to make bad choices. In addition, remember that sin includes not only your wrong *actions* but also your wrong *thoughts*. This is why you are called to guard your mind—so that you can walk worthy of your calling.

Philippians 4:8 holds the key to using the helmet of salvation effectively in order to protect your mind and your thought life:

> And now, dear brothers and sisters, let me say one more thing. . . . Fix your thoughts on what is true and honorable and right. Think about things that are pure and lovely and admirable. Think about things that are excellent and worthy of praise.
>
> —NLT

These are the types of things that you are to think about and dwell on. If something is *not* true, honorable, right, pure, lovely, admirable, excellent, and worthy of praise, you should *not* be thinking about it, and you should especially *not* be dwelling on it! Keep your thoughts away from anything that pollutes your mind. If you begin to think on discouraging, disgusting, and/or polluted things—change your thinking! This may take some practice at first, and you may have to change your thinking hundreds of times a day. But as you do, you will be wearing your helmet of salvation.

What does the helmet of salvation protect?

_____

_____

_____

What can your thoughts trigger?

_____

_____

_____

What can you do to protect your thought life?

_____

_____

_____

The sword of the Spirit is the next piece of equipment in the Christian's arsenal. Like the belt of truth, it also represents the Word of God, but there is an important distinction. In the New Testament, there are two Greek words used to describe the Word: *logos* and *rhema*. *Logos* speaks of the general knowledge of the Word, which represents the belt of truth. *Rhema*, on the other hand, speaks of specific words or phrases. It is the piercing, double-edged sword of the Spirit that defines specific truths and allows you to apply these truths when Satan attempts to attack you. It is more than a general knowledge of the Word of God—it is a precise weapon, meant to yield the truth of God's Word in specific situations to help you overcome temptations. This is why it is vitally important to read God's Word and to memorize key verses, so that you will know how to use this incredible weapon.

Psalm 119:11 holds the key to effectively using the sword of the Spirit:

> I have hidden your word in my heart that I might not sin against you.

As you take the time to memorize God's Word, you are actually hiding it within your heart. Then, when you find yourself in a situation in which you are being tempted, God will bring His Word to your memory. All of a sudden, a verse will come to you for that specific situation. At the moment you take action based on God's Word, you will be using the sword of the Spirit effectively.

What does the sword of the Spirit represent?

_____

_____

_____

How do you hide God's Word in your heart so that you are prepared to use the sword of the Spirit?

_____

_____

_____

The weapon of *prayer* is perhaps one of the most important weapons that you can use to be victorious. Through prayer, you can receive God's strength and guidance to walk worthy of your calling in any situation. However, you have to make the choice to use this weapon. As Charles Spurgeon wrote, "Look upward, and let us weep. O God, You have given us a mighty weapon, and we have permitted it to rust."[3] Do not allow the mighty weapon of prayer to lay still and rust. Instead, use it every time you find yourself in a situation that you need God's strength and guidance. Prayer is a top-secret weapon that God has equipped you with for the battle, so that you can live out who you are in Christ in a *practical* manner.

Prayer is a top-secret weapon!

I once watched an interesting movie called *Windtalkers,* which was inspired by the true story of the Navajo soldiers whose courage and sacrifices helped the United States to win the Second World War in the Pacific.[4] In war, communication is of the greatest importance. Without communication, the battle will be lost. The Americans knew this fact, so they went to great lengths to develop and protect a secret code that the enemy could not decipher. The code they developed was based on the Navajo Indian language, and it was a vital component in their victory in every major battle in the Pacific.[5] The code, which was never broken, was a top-secret communication weapon that helped the Americans win the war.[6]

You can learn much from the Americans' victory in the Pacific. You are also in the middle of a battlefield, and the only way for you to be able to fight the good fight and be victorious in the Lord's army is by having direct communication with your commander, God.[7] He desires to direct every step you take, so that you can walk worthy of your calling.

First Thessalonians 5:16–18 teaches about this mighty weapon of prayer:

> Rejoice always; *pray without ceasing*; in everything give thanks; for this is God's will for you in Christ Jesus.
> —NASB, emphasis added

You are called to pray without ceasing. This means that it is important to pray always and about everything. You can have a constant, silent conversation with God in your mind, asking Him to lead and guide you.

Through prayer, you receive God's strength, guidance, and wisdom for every situation, trial, and temptation in life. Through prayer, you receive His strength to fight the good fight. Through prayer, you receive His guidance to be victorious. And through prayer, you receive His wisdom to walk worthy of your calling. Remember, He loves you more than you know. He desires to be your best friend, your all-in-all, and the lover of your soul. He has given you this mighty weapon of prayer as a top-secret weapon to win the battle. As you pray and seek Him in all situations, trials, and temptations, you will be using the weapon of prayer effectively.

Have you allowed the mighty weapon of prayer to rust?

_____

_____

_____

What does it mean to pray without ceasing?

_____

_____

_____

What can you receive through prayer?

_____

_____

_____

I pray you will choose to pick up the armor of God. Remember, you are able to fight the good fight. You are able to be victorious and walk worthy of your calling. You are able to be a light unto Him and reflect His glory. You are able to be strong in the Lord—strong until the end. So, in view of all that you have learned in this chapter, pick up the armor of God and determine in your heart and your mind to walk worthy of who you are in Christ, so that you may *go in peace!*

DIGGING DEEPER

In this chapter, you learned many truths about who you are in Christ. Take some time this week to look up the following verses. Underline or highlight them in your Bible, and then write out any that are special in a journal or on a 3×5 card so that you will have them close at hand when you need encouragement.

You are able to fight the good fight—1 Timothy 6:11–14; 2 Timothy 4:7

You are able to be victorious—Psalm 18:35; Psalm 60:12; Psalm 108:13; Psalm 118:15; Romans 16:20

You are able to walk worthy of your position in Christ—Colossians 1:9–14

You are able to reflect the King's glory—2 Corinthians 3:18

You are equipped with the armor of God—Ephesians 6:10–18

You are called to pray without ceasing—1 Thessalonians 5:17

You are strong till the end—1 Corinthians 1:8; Jude 1:24–25

CHAPTER EIGHT

HOPE AND
A FUTURE

Y ou have learned some amazing, life-changing principles as you read this book. If you choose to continue to apply them to your life each day, you will become all that God intends for you to be. In this chapter, I want to share seven practical ways for you to stand firm and walk worthy of your calling—practical ways that I wish someone would have been brave enough to share with me when I was a teen. However, before we do this, let's look a bit more closely at what it means to be *sanctified*. First Thessalonians 4:3–8 teaches the following:

> It is God's will that you should be sanctified: that you should avoid sexual immorality; that each of you should learn to control his [or her] own body in a way that is holy and honorable, not in passionate lust like the heathen, who do not know God; and that in this matter no one should wrong his brother [or sister] or take advantage of him [or her]. The Lord will punish men for all such sins,

as we have already told you and warned you. For God did not call us to be impure, but to live a holy life. Therefore, he [or she] who rejects this instruction does not reject man but God, who gives you his Holy Spirit.

When I was a teen, I think the youth leaders were afraid to mention the word *sex*. I think they thought that if they talked about it, we might do it. I don't know why they were afraid. God's Word talks about sex, which shows that we also need to talk about it. In fact, in my many years of discipling, I have found that Satan often uses sexual immorality to destroy the intimate relationship between a believer and God.

You are set apart to live your life differently!

You are called to live a holy life, so it is important that you do not reject His instruction. It is God's will that you should be sanctified—that you should avoid sexual immorality. In chapter 6, we discussed how being *sanctified* means to be set apart and to be free from sin. We also looked at the *positional aspect* and the *practical aspect* of sanctification. We discussed how from the moment you accepted Jesus Christ as your Lord and Savior, you were set apart positionally and that because of this, you are called to live your life differently than everyone else. In view of this truth, it is time for you to learn how to live out the practical aspect of your sanctification, so that you can make choices that will keep you free from sin and give you a hope and a future.

Now, God did not make a bunch of rules so that your life would not be any fun. Instead, He made His commands and decrees out of His love for you. He knows what will hurt you and what will cause you pain. He is the one who created sexual intimacy. He created it to be something beautiful, but only within the boundaries of marriage. When He set Adam and Eve in the Garden of Eden, they were both naked, but they felt no shame.[1] Within the boundaries of marriage, when both the husband and wife are walking worthy of their calling, there is no heartache and sin. Instead, there is love, acceptance, peace, and contentment. Deuteronomy 10:12–13 teaches why God set His commands and decrees:

> And now, O Israel, what does the LORD your God ask of you but to fear the LORD your God, to walk in all his ways, to love him, to serve the LORD your God with all your heart and with all your soul, and to observe the LORD's commands and decrees that I am giving you today *for your own good?* (emphasis added).

What are the five things that God asks of you in the above passage?

1. _____
2. _____
3. _____
4. _____
5. _____

According to the above passage, why does God ask this of you?

_____

_____

_____

God loves you deeply and wants the absolute best for you. He does not make these rules to take away your fun—that's just a lie Satan whispers in your ear. God asks you to follow His commands and decrees for *your own good!* As you follow His commands and decrees, you will live out who you are in Christ *practically* and have hope and a future. Let's look a bit more closely at why He wants you to avoid sexual immorality. In Ezekiel 16:4–8, God declares the following:

> On the day you were born your cord was not cut, nor were you washed with water to make you clean, nor were you rubbed with salt or wrapped in cloths. No one looked on you with pity or had compassion enough to do any of these things for you. Rather, you were thrown out into the open field, for on the day you were born you were despised.
>
> Then I passed by and saw you kicking about in your blood, and as you lay there in your blood I said to you, "Live!" I made you grow like a plant of the field. You grew up and developed and became the most beautiful of jewels. Your breasts were formed and your hair grew, you who were naked and bare.
>
> Later I passed by, and when I looked at you and saw that you were old enough for love, I spread the corner of my garment over you and covered your nakedness. I gave you my solemn oath and entered into a covenant with you, declares the Sovereign LORD, and you became mine.

These verses describe much of what you have already learned in this book. In Ezekiel 16:4, God says, "On the day you were born your cord was not cut." As we discussed in chapter 2, although you were created in the image and likeness of God, you were born in the image and likeness of Adam. This is why you struggle with sin! God goes on to say, "Nor were you washed with water . . . nor were you rubbed with salt . . . for on the day you were born you were despised" (Ezekiel 16:4–5). You were despised because of your tie to Adam and sin!

But then, God says that He "passed by and saw you kicking about in your blood, and as you lay there in your blood [He] said to you, 'Live!'" (Ezekiel 16:6). This is the miracle. After the downward spiral of sin, sin, and more sin had led you into the miry pit, God looked on you in love and pulled you out. As He reached out His hand and you made the choice to accept it, He said, "Live!" The moment you accepted His precious gift of salvation, He began His work in your life.

He reached out His hand!

God then says, "I made you grow like a plant of the field. You grew up and developed and became the most beautiful of jewels. Your breasts were formed and your hair grew, you who were naked and bare" (Ezekiel 16:7). This describes not only how you grow spiritually—"You grew up and developed and became the most beautiful of jewels" (Ezekiel 16:7)—but also physically—"Your breasts were formed and your hair grew, you who were naked and bare" (Ezekiel 16:7). Because of this, listen to what God declares: "Later I passed by, and when I looked at you and saw that you were old enough for love, I spread the corner of my garment over you and covered your nakedness" (Ezekiel 16:8).

God says that He spread the corner of His garment over you and covered your nakedness. What God has covered, let no one—male or female—uncover in any manner until the night of your wedding. This is the part of His plan that will keep you free from shame and all of the other cruddy consequences that you learned about earlier during your years of singleness.

> The man and his wife were both naked, and they felt no shame.
>
> —Genesis 2:25

And this is the part of His plan for your future. God wants the absolute best for you. He wants to give you a hope and a future. He wants you to be able to stand before your spouse, on your wedding night, with no shame.

> "For I know the plans I have for you," declares the LORD, "plans to prosper you and not to harm you, plans to give you hope and a future."
>
> —Jeremiah 29:11

In the passage in Ezekiel, God goes on to say:

> I gave you my solemn oath and entered into a covenant with you . . . and you became mine.
>
> —Ezekiel 16:8

God entered into a covenant with you, and you became His the moment you accepted Him. He is a jealous God, and He does not want to share you with anyone until the day you are married. Then, He will share you with your spouse, because God's Word says that a man and a woman become one flesh. Genesis 2:24 declares this truth:

> For this reason a man will leave his father and mother and be united to his wife, and they will become one flesh.

God looks at a husband and a wife as one. It's the way He has designed it. In fact, He wants husbands and wives to be fruitful and multiply. That's why He created sexual intimacy to be so enjoyable. There is nothing wrong with sex within the boundaries of marriage.

But beware! Everything that God makes beautiful, Satan wants to destroy. This is why Satan will tempt you to have sex outside of marriage. Yes, it feels good—there is pleasure in sin for a short season. But then comes destruction. That is why God tells you not to live your life by your feelings, but by the truth of His Word. He wants you to stand firm and live a holy life, so that you can be all that He intends you to be, and have a hope and a future.

In view of this hope, God proclaimed,

> I gave you my solemn oath and entered into a covenant with you, declares the Sovereign LORD, and you became mine.
>
> —Ezekiel 16:8

A *covenant* is a formal and binding agreement.[2] One example of a covenant that God made with mankind is found in the story of the flood in Genesis. At that time, God was greatly grieved over man's wickedness and sin. So He decided to wipe out mankind—everyone except for Noah and his family.

> Noah was a righteous man, blameless among the people of his time, and he walked with God.
>
> —Genesis 6:9

God told Noah of His plan to wipe out mankind and called him to build an ark. This is a different ark from the one you learned about in chapter 6. That was the Ark of the Covenant, which was an important piece of furniture located in the Holy of Holies. In this case, the ark was a huge ship. After Noah built the ark, God flooded and destroyed the whole earth. When the water receded, God made a covenant with Noah and with all of his descendants—which includes you and me—and said,

> I establish my covenant with you: Never again will all life be cut off by the waters of a flood; never again will there be a flood to destroy the earth.
>
> —Genesis 9:11

God has been faithful to His promise. Never again has He sent a flood to destroy the whole earth.

Let's go back to the verses in Ezekiel that talk about covenant. In Ezekiel 16:8, God states,

> When I looked at you and saw that you were old enough for love, I spread the corner of my garment over you and covered your nakedness. I gave you my solemn oath and entered into a covenant with you . . . and you became mine.

As a teen, your body has developed and, in most cases, you are old enough, physically, for love, but God is saying that He has entered into a covenant with you. The word *covenant* is used symbolically in this verse. It is symbolic of entering into a marriage covenant; or, in other words, a marriage contract.[3]

According to God's Word, you are His bride. Now, I know that this concept will be a little strange for the guys, but basically what God's Word is saying is that you are set apart for God and God alone. He is a jealous God. He has covered you and does not want anyone to uncover what He has covered. He knows that any sexual relationship outside of marriage will eventually cause you hurt and pain. Remember, He wants only the best for you and has established His commands and decrees for your own good.

Now, before we look at the seven practical ways to walk worthy of our calling, we need to discuss one more thing. You need to know that, even if you have already fallen into the sin of sexual immorality, you can still become sanctified and live a holy life for God. First Corinthians 6:9–11 bears repeating:

> Do you not know that the wicked will not inherit the kingdom of God? Do not be deceived: Neither the sexually immoral . . . nor adulterers nor male prostitutes nor homosexual offenders . . . will inherit the kingdom of God. . . . And that is what some of you *were*. But you were washed, you were sanctified, you were justified in the name of the Lord Jesus Christ and by the Spirit of our God (emphasis added).

Repent! Change your way!

Notice that Paul does not say that if you have been sexually active outside of marriage, that's it! You're done! You'll be zapped! No! He says, "that is what some of you *were*"—past tense! The moment you admit your sin to yourself, confess it to God, and repent of it, you are sanctified. From that moment on, you are called to live a holy life. Therefore, know that if you have been sexually active, God does not want you to stay in your sinful lifestyle. You need to admit your sin of sexual immorality and confess it to God. (Remember, He already knows what you have been doing. Nothing is hidden from Him. He simply wants you to confess it to Him.) Then you need to repent and change your ways! Stop doing what you have been doing wrong and get right with God. No matter what your sin is—even the sin of sexual immorality—admit it, confess it, and repent of it so that your intimate relationship with God may be restored.

With this in mind, let's learn seven practical ways to live a holy life, so that you will have hope and a future.

The first practical way is to *live according to God's Word*. You can apply this principle to any situation in your life. Psalm 119:9–11 states,

> How can a young man [or woman] keep his [or her] way pure? By living according to your word. I seek you with all my heart: do not let me stray from your commands. I have hidden your word in my heart that I might not sin against you.

According to this passage in Psalms, how can a young person keep his or her way pure? What are the four things listed in the passage?

1. _____

2. _____

3. _____

4. _____

To fully understand this first practical way to live a holy life, let's look at each of the four things you listed above. First, you are called to *live according to God's Word*. Learn God's Word and make wises choices based upon its truth. As you do, if you remember from the last chapter, this means wearing the belt of truth.

Second, you are called to *seek God with all your heart.* Do this by spending time with Him each day in the Holy of Holies. Remember you will find God's strength, guidance, and wisdom for every situation in life in the Holy of Holies.

Third, you are called to *not stray from His commands.* Make

Make wise choices!

wise choices based on God's Word, and on who you are in Christ—which, as we discussed, means wearing the breastplate of righteousness. You are a child of the King. God has a plan for your life, to give you hope and a future. Do not settle for second best.

Fourth, you are called to *hide God's Word in your heart.* As you memorize key verses that speak to your heart, God will bring them to your memory at just the right moment. When Satan bombards you with his lies, God will bring a verse or passage into your memory to strengthen you and show you how to live a holy life according to His Word. Remember, this is effectively using the sword of the Spirit. It's so cool. I challenge you to check it out! Try it! God is faithful! When you do this, you live out who you are in Christ *practically.*

The second practical way to live a holy life is to *choose your friends wisely.* Like most people, you have a desire to feel loved and accepted. This is normal. But Satan will use your feelings and desires to cause you to lower your guard. Many times, your friends can influence you to do things that you know in your heart are wrong. Proverbs 12:26 teaches this important practicality:

> The righteous should choose his friends carefully, For the way of the wicked leads them astray.
>
> —NKJV

First Corinthians 15:33 repeats God's warning:

> Do not be misled: "Bad company corrupts good character."

In view of God's warning, remember to live by the truth of who you are in Christ. You are loved. You are the bride of Christ. You have hope and a future. This is true whether you feel it or not. So choose friends who won't lead you astray. When you do this, you are living out who you are in Christ *practically*.

The third practical way to live a holy life is to *avoid alcohol and drugs*. Ephesians 5:17–18 states,

> Therefore do not be foolish, but understand what the Lord's will is. Do not get drunk on wine, which leads to debauchery. Instead, be filled with the Spirit.

Satan wants you caught in the vicious downward spiral!

Debauchery means "excessive indulgence in sensual pleasure; seduction from duty, allegiance, or virtue."[4] *Seduction* means "enticing someone astray from right behavior."[5] When you are under the influence of alcohol or drugs, it can lead to debauchery. You can get into a situation in which you let your guard down and do something that you would never have done if you were sober.

Satan knows this and will use this against you. He will entice you away from right behavior. He wants you to get caught in the vicious downward spiral of sin, sin, and more sin, and he wants to take away your hope and future. If you choose this foolish path, it will lead to depression, anxiety, and all of the other cruddy consequences you learned about in previous chapters.

Let me share a true story of a teen who didn't choose her friends wisely or follow God's warning. One day her best friend, who didn't share her values, wanted to go hang out at the beach. Her best friend had a boyfriend who wanted to come along and bring his friend. This girl had never met the boyfriend's friend, but she wanted to have fun, and so she agreed to go and make it a foursome.

As the sun began to set, they began to party and drink beer. Soon, her best friend headed down the beach with her boyfriend, leaving this girl alone with the guy she hardly knew. She felt nervous, so she began to drink more beer to calm her nerves. One thing led to another, and soon Satan was at work. The girl was seduced from what she knew was right.

This girl had determined in her heart and mind to remain pure until marriage. But she had not protected herself from getting into a situation beyond her control, and her actions led to debauchery. The next morning, she woke up in a fog and couldn't remember everything that had happened. But at school the next day, the boy spread tales and told everyone about his night with her on the beach. She was devastated.

Instead of immediately confessing her sin and getting her heart right with God—for God is faithful and just to forgive us our sins no matter what they are—this young girl allowed Satan to have a stronghold and use the guilt of her sin against her. A few months later, she met a guy

Soon she was caught up in the vicious downward spiral of sin, sin, and more sin!

whom she really liked. Soon, he was pressuring her to have sex with him. In her heart, she didn't want to give in. She still wanted to wait until marriage. But Satan began whispering his lies in her ear. "Remember the night on the beach? How can you say you want to wait? What a hypocrite! You say one thing and do another."

On and on, Satan condemned her and used her unconfessed sin against her. The girl was soon caught up in the vicious downward spiral of sin, sin, and more sin. She decided to sleep with her boyfriend, only to find out later that she was still a virgin! That night on the beach, she had passed out from the beer. The boy she hardly knew had lied to everyone at school. But now she had given away a precious gift she had wanted to keep for her future husband. And it was all because she didn't walk worthy of her calling and didn't live out the practical aspect of who she was in Christ.

If this girl had chosen her friends wisely and said no to drinking that night on the beach, this would never have happened. She would have saved herself years of heartache and pain. Do not allow Satan to entice you from right behavior by hanging out with the wrong crowd, or by drinking or doing drugs. If you do, you are only setting yourself up to stumble and fall. Instead, remember to stand firm. If you find yourself in a situation that is getting out of control—leave! Have your feet shod with the preparation of the gospel of peace. Let your actions speak louder than your words.

My daughters always knew that if they found themselves in an uncomfortable situation, they could call me and I would immediately come and get them. Make these same arrangements with someone who loves you. Memorize their phone number in case you don't have your cell phone, and call them if needed. It could actually save your life! As you make wise choices about your friends and avoid alcohol and drugs, you are living out who you are in Christ *practically.*

The fourth practical way to live a holy life is to *not be unequally yoked.* The word *yoked* means "to be or become joined, linked, or united."[6] *Unequal* means "not of the same quality, value, rank, [or] ability."[7] In other words, you are not to become unequally united with someone who does not have your same beliefs and values. If you become involved with someone who does not love God with all his or her heart and mind, there will eventually be a battle (a *huge* battle) over who is going to be first in your life—that person or God. Second Corinthians 6:14a states this clearly:

Do not be unequally yoked together with unbelievers.

—NKJV

God knows your future. His Word says that He has:

Called [you] to a holy life—not because of anything [you] have done but because of his own purpose and grace.

—2 Timothy 1:9

You are called to live a holy life because He has a purpose and a plan for your life—a plan that will give you hope and a future. Therefore, when you feel tempted to start a relationship with someone who does not love the Lord as deeply as you do, STOP! You are called to walk by faith and not by sight. God already knows who your spouse will be, if you are to marry, so have faith in God and be patient. Pick up your shield of faith and trust God. He will bring the right person into your life in His perfect timing. Instead of getting involved in a relationship that will only cause you hurt and pain, enjoy this time of singleness and allow God to be your all-in-all, your best friend, the lover of your soul. As you do, you will be living out who you are in Christ *practically*. That's His desire for your life. Remember, He is a jealous God.

The fifth practical way to live a holy life is to *avoid temptation*. There will be temptations. But God has provided a way out so that you can stand up under any temptation and remain firm. First Corinthians 10:13 states,

> No temptation has seized you except what is common to man. And God is faithful; he will not let you be tempted beyond what you can bear. But when you are tempted, he will also provide a way out so that you can stand up under it.

One way to avoid temptation is by protecting what you look at and not allowing your mind to be polluted by Satan's lies. In the Bible, Job was described as being "blameless and upright; he feared God and shunned evil" (Job 1:1). In Job 31:1, he states,

> I made a covenant with my eyes not to look lustfully at a girl.

Job realized that what he looked at affected what he thought about. Because of this, he promised himself that he would not allow his eyes to look at something that would cause him to stumble and fall.

Girls aren't exempt from this one! Even girls can stumble and fall by what they look at and especially by what they allow their thoughts to dwell on. Girls, think about it. What do you read? What do you watch on television? What music do you listen to? Do any of these things bring ungodly images into your mind? If so, they can entice your feelings of loneliness or your desire to be loved.

It is more than a causal glance!

Remember the story of Adam and Eve in chapter 3?

> When the woman *saw* that the fruit of the tree was good for food and pleasing to the eye . . . she took some and ate it.
>
> —Genesis 3:6

The sin began when Eve looked at the fruit for some time and considered eating it. When she *saw* that the fruit was good, this was more than a causal glance—it was something that she *chose* to consider and think about. As we discussed, the same is true for you and me. Sin first takes root when we begin to look intently at something that we know is wrong. Then we begin to think about it and consider it. If we do not stop our thoughts, we can begin down the vicious spiral of sin, sin, and more sin.

So be warned. Be careful about what you look at and what you allow your thoughts to dwell on. What you are going through is not uncommon to man, and God has already provided "a way out so that you can stand up under it" (1 Corinthians 10:13). It is what you do when faced with temptation that will set you apart. So change your thinking and equip yourself with the helmet of salvation. As you change your thinking, you will be living out who you are in Christ *practically*.

The sixth practical way to live a holy life is to *not conform to the pattern of the world*. Romans 12:2 states,

> Do not conform any longer to the pattern of this world, but be transformed by the renewing of your mind. Then you will be able to test and approve what God's will is—his good, pleasing and perfect will.

This verse in Romans states it pretty clearly: Follow God and His Word, and not the ways of the world. Just because everyone is doing something doesn't mean that you need to join in. If everyone were jumping off a cliff to their death, would you follow them? Do not conform to the pattern of the world. Remember, people are watching you to see what makes your life different. Just because everyone has a boyfriend or a girlfriend doesn't mean that you have to have one, especially if you are not old enough or are not ready to get married. Remember, you are the bride of Christ. So be content in His love and, if it is in His plan, He will bring your spouse to you in His perfect timing. As you refuse to conform to the patterns of this world and live your life in such a way as to be a light unto God, you will be living out who you are in Christ *practically*.

The seventh and final practical way to live a holy life is to *pray*. Proverbs 3:6 teaches,

> In all your ways acknowledge him, and he will make your paths straight.

No matter where you are or what is taking place around you, take time to meet with God in the Holy of Holies. Seek Him in any and every situation. Acknowledge your ways to Him and ask Him to guide you every step of the way.

A Holy of Holies Christian seeks God with every choice in life—big and small. They ask, "Lord, what is *Your* will in this situation? Do You want me to go here? Do You want me to do that?" If you truly seek God in prayer and are willing to listen, He will be faithful to impress on your heart what He wants you to do in any and every situation. Remember, prayer is an important piece of your spiritual equipment. As you pick up your weapon of prayer, you will discover God's plan and purpose for your life, and this will give you hope and a future. As you pick up your weapon of prayer, you will also be living out who you are in Christ *practically*.

Let's briefly recap the seven practical ways to walk worthy of your calling and live a holy life:

1. Live according to God's Word
2. Choose your friends wisely
3. Do not drink alcohol or do drugs
4. Do not be unequally yoked
5. Avoid temptation
6. Do not conform to the patterns of this world
7. Pray

After looking at these seven practical ways to walk worthy of your calling, are there any that you need to improve on? If so, which ones?

_____

_____

_____

What can you do to improve in these areas?

_____

_____

_____

James 1:22 teaches,

> Do not merely listen to the word, and so deceive yourselves. *Do what it says* (emphasis added).

It is as simple as that! Do what God's Word says!

In 1 Corinthians 6:13–20, Paul wraps up what we have discussed in this chapter very clearly:

> The body is not meant for sexual immorality, but for the Lord, and the Lord for the body. . . . Do you not know that your bodies are members of Christ himself? Shall I then take the members of Christ and unite them with a prostitute? Never! Do you not know that he who unites himself with a prostitute is one with her in body. For it is said, "The two will become one flesh." But he who unites himself with the Lord is one with him in spirit.
>
> Flee from sexual immorality. All other sins a man commits are outside his body, but he who sins sexually sins against his own body. Do you not know that your body is a temple of the Holy Spirit, who is in you, whom you have received from God? You are not your own; you were bought at a price. Therefore honor God with your body.

God has set you apart. You are the temple of the Holy Spirit. He desires to give you hope and a future, but you will only discover that hope and future by following His will for your life. It is God's will that you are sanctified—that you avoid sexual immorality. However, He loves you so deeply that He gives you the

The choice is yours! What will you choose?

choice to follow Him or the choice to live by your feelings and fleshly desires. What will you choose?

The Bible describes both Noah and Job as blameless. This does not mean that they were without sin, but that they determined in their hearts and minds to walk worthy of their calling. They determined to be all that God intended for them to be. They determined in their hearts and minds to live out the *practical aspect* of who God was calling them to be and follow His commands regardless of what others thought. First Corinthians 1:8 declares:

> He will keep you strong to the end, so that you will be blameless on the day of our Lord Jesus Christ.

After God made a covenant with Noah and his descendents to never again destroy the whole earth by flood, He gave a sign to mankind to remind them of His promise. The sign He gave was the rainbow:

> And God said, "This is the sign of the covenant I am making between me and you and every living creature with you, a covenant for all generations to come: I have set my rainbow in the clouds, and it will be the sign of the covenant between me and the earth."
>
> —Genesis 9:12–13

God made a covenant with you the moment you accepted Him as your Lord and Savior. You can also make a covenant with Him and *choose* this day to remain sexually pure until you are married. Remember, it doesn't matter what you did last week, yesterday or even one hour ago—don't let Satan have a stronghold by using your past sins against you. You can choose today to walk worthy of your calling and be all that God intends you to be.

So take some quiet time and spend it with God. Meet with Him in the Holy of Holies. Pour out your heart to Him. Then, if you choose to do so, make a covenant with Him from this moment on to remain pure until marriage. You can even find a token as a sign of your decision. When my daughters decided in their hearts to remain pure until marriage, their father and I gave them both a purity ring as a reminder of their covenant with God. The ring helped to remind them every day of their covenant. You can also find a similar token to help you stand firm.

God loves you more than you know. He truly does have a hope and a future planned for you. Never forget that you are the temple of the Holy Spirit. You are to stand firm. For you are called to live a holy life so that you can be all that God intends you to be. As you do, you will have hope and a future, which will enable you to *go in peace!*

DIGGING DEEPER

If you desire to be all that God intends you to be, spend some quiet time with Him to sit at His feet in the Holy of Holies and write whatever He puts on your heart. He wants to speak with you. Then make a choice today to either walk according to God's Word and remain pure until marriage, or conform to the patterns of this world and be just like everyone else. If you choose to remain pure until marriage, make a covenant with God and find some kind of token to help you remember your covenant.

In this chapter, you learned many truths of who you are in Christ. Take some time this week to look up the verses on the following page and underline or highlight them in your Bible. Then write down any that are special to you in a journal or on a 3×5 card, so that you can memorize them and have them close at hand when you need encouragement.

You are to stand firm—Exodus 14:13–14;
  1 Corinthians 15:58; 16:13; Ephesians 6:13–14
You are called to live a holy life—1 Thessalonians 4:3–8;
  2 Timothy 1:9
You are able to be all that God intends you to be, which
  will give you hope and a future—Jeremiah 29:11
You are the bride of Christ—Isaiah 62:5; Ezekiel 16:8;
  Revelation 19:7
You are set apart for God and God alone—
  Deuteronomy 4:24
You are called to live according to God's Word—
  Psalm 119:9–11
You are called to seek God with all your heart—
  Psalm 70:4; 119:9–10; Luke 12:31; Hebrews 11:6
You are called to not stray from His commands—
  Joshua 1:7; Psalm 119:9–10
You are called to hide God's Word in your heart—
  Joshua 1:8; Psalm 119:9–10; Proverbs 2:1–22; 7:1–3
You are to walk by faith—2 Corinthians 5:7
You are able to stand up under temptation—
  1 Corinthians 10:13
You are the temple of the Holy Spirit—
  1 Corinthians 6:18–20
You are blameless—Psalm 19:13; Proverbs 11:20;
  1 Corinthians 1:8; Ephesians 1:4; 2 Peter 3:14

CHAPTER NINE

YOU ARE CHOSEN

Before we begin this chapter, let's take a look at how God has worked in your life. Turn to the section titled "Goals" that you filled out in the Introduction. Read the goals you wrote and write "yes" next to any goal that God has helped you to meet.

In reviewing your goals, did God work in your life? If so, how?

_____

_____

_____

Were most of your goals answered?

_____

_____

_____

Were you surprised?

_____

_____

_____

In my many years of discipling, I have seen that God truly does work in a person's life to help him or her meet these goals. Usually, about 90 percent of a person's goals have been met by the time he or she gets to this place in the book. The other 10 percent are typically goals such as, "I want to be used by God to help others," or, "I want my life to have purpose and meaning." Only time will tell if these goals will be met, but this does not mean that God has not answered the person's request. It just means that these are goals for the future. What is really wonderful about these types of goals is that God desires them as well! In fact, He has called each of us to help others, which will cause us to live a life of purpose and meaning.

But what does it mean to be called by God? In this statement, the word *called* has a couple of different meanings. First, it can mean "a summons or invitation."[1] A wonderful example of this is when God *called* you to Himself with His loving kindness so that you would receive His invitation to be saved. The second meaning of *called* is "a strong inner urge or prompting."[2] This occurs when God puts something on your heart that you feel compelled to act on.

What are the two meanings of "called"?

1. _____

2. _____

So, a *calling* is a summons, a desire, or an urging by the Holy Spirit to do something. As you follow the urging of the Holy Spirit, your life will be of worth. You will come to the end of your life and know that your life had purpose and meaning. You will know that you were all that God intended you to be.

According to God's Word, your calling is a worthy call. It is a call to live a holy life. It is a call to stand true to the gospel of grace. It is a call to fellowship that will affect your relationships, but at the same time, it is a call to submit to those whom God has placed over you. It is a call to treat people with God's love as you overcome evil with good and repay insult with blessing—something you can only do if you rely on God for wisdom and power. It is a call to stand firm in the midst of trials and temptations. It is a call to which you are forever bound and cannot change. It is a call to step out of the darkness and into the hope of God's wonderful light. It is a call to have peace in your heart, which will allow you to *go in peace.* It is an upward call; a call toward heaven. In fact, you are to make your calling sure. Therefore, you are not to take your calling lightly.

You may have noticed that your call is an interpersonal one—a call for relationship and fellowship with others. Yet this is often where problems arise, for it is in your interpersonal relationships that you have the possibility of getting hurt. This can bring you back to where you were when you started this book—chewing the cud and spitting the consequences. God does not want you to go back to who you were. He wants you to change and experience the hope that He has promised. You are His work of art, and He wants to mold you and make you into the person He intends you to be. He has called you and chosen you to bear fruit. As Jesus said in John 15:16,

You did not choose me, but I chose you and appointed you
to go and bear fruit—fruit that will last.

God constantly wants you to be in change mode. He wants
you to become more and more like Him each day, and reflect
His glory to those around you so that you will bear fruit. He
wants you to be an ambassador for Christ. Being an *ambassador for Christ* simply means that you are Christ's representative
here on earth. Remember, actions speak louder than words.
As the apostle Paul declares in 2 Corinthians 5:20,

> We are therefore Christ's ambassadors, as though God
> were making his appeal through us.

This is why you were called. This is why you were chosen.
As Ephesians 4:1–2 states,

> *I urge you to live a life worthy of the calling you have received.*
> Be completely humble and gentle; be patient, bearing with
> one another in love (emphasis added).

So I encourage you to walk worthy
of your calling so that you will bear
fruit.

So, how do you live your life
worthy of your calling? Many times,
God will place you into situations
and trials that will develop your
character. He will use the people
around you to mold you into the
person He desires you to be, so that
you will mature to the point at which
you can bear fruit. Often, He uses
a prickly person to accomplish His

It can be pretty painful
to hug a cactus!

will in our lives. A *prickly person* is someone who is hard to deal with—someone who is hard to love. Think of the prickly thorns on a cactus. It can be pretty painful to hug a cactus.

Maybe the prickly person in your life is one of your parents. God calls you to:

> "Honor your father and mother"—which is the first commandment with a promise—"that it may go well with you and that you may enjoy long life on the earth."
> —Ephesians 6:2–3

Maybe the prickly person in your life is your boss. God calls you to do your work to the best of your ability:

> Whatever you do, work at it with all your heart, as working for the Lord, not for men.
> —Colossians 3:23

Maybe the prickly person in your life is your neighbor. God calls you to

> Love your neighbor as yourself.
> —Matthew 19:19

One definition of *neighbor* is "fellow man."[3] So this means that you need to love anyone whom God puts around you, not just the person who lives next door.

Do you have a prickly person in your life? Do you have someone who is hard to get along with or difficult to love? If so, who?

_____

_____

_____

What is it about that person that makes it so hard to get along with him or her?

_____

_____

_____

So how can you live your life worthy of your calling when you have prickly people to deal with? How can you be completely humble, gentle, patient, and loving? How can you bear fruit when these individuals are so difficult to get along with? How can you be Christ's representative on earth when they create difficult situations?

You can find the answers to these questions within some interesting paradoxes. These paradoxes will keep you from cud-chewing and consequence-spitting so that you can *go in peace*. A *paradox* is "a statement that seems self-contradictory but may be true."[4] *Contradictory* means "opposing, conflicting or at odds with each other." In other words, a *paradox* is a statement that contains two ideas that are completely opposite of each other, each of which may still be true. And one interesting definition of *paradox* is "a statement that seems contrary to common sense and yet is perhaps true."[5] So a paradox may even seem to go against our common sense.

The Christian life is filled with paradoxes. Let me give you some examples of just a few of the paradoxes that you are called to discover in your Christian life:

- When we are weak, we are strong.[6]
- Those who are poor are rich.[7]
- The first will be last, and the last will be first.[8]

- We must die to self in order to live.[9]
- When you give, you receive.[10]

In Matthew 16:24–25, Jesus explained another important paradox:

> If anyone would come after me, he must deny himself and take up his cross and follow me. For *whoever wants to save his life will lose it, but whoever loses his life for me will find it* (emphasis added).

To understand this paradox, we must first understand what Jesus meant when He said, "If anyone would come after me, he must deny himself and take up his cross and follow me." Within this statement, there are three principles that Jesus is calling us to live by so that we can discover the key to the paradox: (1) we must deny self, (2) we must take up our cross, and (3) we must follow Christ.

What are the three principles that Jesus calls us to live by?

1. _____

2. _____

3. _____

Let's look at each of these principles. *Denying self* means that you must give up anything you desire or want that keeps you from doing the will of God. Now, don't misunderstand—this does not necessarily mean that if you want something, it is wrong or a sin. It simply means that Jesus must be first in your life. If there is any *thing* that you are placing before Jesus, you need to let that *thing* go in your heart.

Let me give you some examples of what this *thing* could be in your life. It might be an actual item that you are placing before God, such as a car, a house, or money. It could be something you are striving for, such as your education, your career, or another goal. It could even be a person, such as a boyfriend or a girlfriend, or an emotion or attitude, such as "I'm right and they're wrong."

Whatever that *thing* is, you cannot place it before God in your heart, for if you do, you have made that *thing* your god. Therefore, when you *deny self*, you deny your selfish feelings and desires and place God and His will *first* in your life. There is only room for one master in your heart. If God is to be first in your life, you must be willing to give up any*thing* in order to place Him in His rightful position.

In Matthew 6:24, Jesus states this clearly:

> No one can serve two masters. Either he will hate the one and love the other, or he will be devoted to the one and despise the other. You cannot serve both God and Money.

In fact, in verse 33 Jesus goes on to say,

> But seek first his kingdom and his righteousness, and all these things will be given to you as well.

As you seek God's kingdom and His righteousness, you deny self and place God in His rightful position in your heart.

This brings us to the second principle: *take up your cross*. To understand the meaning of this phrase, we first need to look at what the cross represents. In Jesus' day, the cross was an instrument of suffering and death. Because of this, many people think that the phrase *take up your cross* means bearing burdens and suffering hardships for the Lord. However, if we consider the context in which Jesus was speaking, we find an even deeper meaning. The phrase *take up your cross* does not just refer to bearing a burden or suffering and carrying a hardship, but also to sacrifice.

In chapter 2, you learned that the wages of sin is death. You deserved the penalty of death for your sins, yet Jesus chose to go to the cross to pay your penalty. For this reason, the cross represents an

Take up your cross!

instrument of sacrifice. Jesus sacrificed His life out of love for you. He suffered and died for you.

In view of this, to *take up your cross* means to give your whole life to God. Just as Jesus gave His whole life for you as a sacrifice, you are to give your whole life to Him as a living sacrifice. Romans 12:1 states this clearly:

> Therefore, I urge you, brothers, in view of God's mercy, *to offer your bodies as living sacrifices,* holy and pleasing to God—this is your spiritual act of worship (emphasis added).

To offer your body as a living sacrifice means that you completely surrender yourself to the will and service of God. As you take up your cross and give your life wholly and completely to God, you will be able to willingly deny self in any and every situation.

This brings us to the third principle: *follow Christ.* To follow Jesus means to live a life that imitates Him. First Peter 2:21 states,

To this you were called, because Christ suffered for you, leaving you an example, that you should follow in his steps.

If you truly desire to be a Holy of Holies Christian, you will ask yourself the question, "What would Jesus do?" in every situation. You will seek God in every decision, big and small. You will desire to deny self and imitate Christ as you put others—even a prickly person—before your own feelings and desires. You will immediately confess and repent of your sins when you fail, because you know that sin breaks fellowship with God and that fellowship with Him gives you the direction you need to follow Jesus. Ephesians 5:1–2 states this clearly:

> Be imitators of God, therefore, as dearly loved children and live a life of love, just as Christ loved us and gave himself up for us as a fragrant offering and sacrifice to God.

Luke 9:23 adds another element to these three principles:

> Then he [Jesus] said to them all: "If anyone would come after me, he must deny himself and take up his cross *daily* and follow me" (emphasis added).

Notice that in Luke's Gospel, the word *daily* is included. This is important, because it implies that choosing to deny self, picking up your cross and following Jesus is not a one-time event, but something that you need to do *daily*—sometimes moment by moment—as you make faith choices verses flesh choices. *Daily*, you need to give your life to God. *Daily*, you need to offer yourself as a living sacrifice to do the will of God. *Daily*, you need to have an attitude that says, "Lord, what do You want from me? I give myself for You, because You gave Yourself for me."

Have you been in a situation recently in which you had to deal with a prickly person?

_____

_____

_____

What happened? Did you live by your feelings and desires, or did you deny self, take up your cross and follow Christ?

_____

_____

_____

If you lived by your feelings and desires, what could you have done differently to be an imitator of Christ?

_____

_____

_____

Once these three principles of denying self, taking up your cross, and following Christ are a part of your daily life, you will get to the place in which you will understand Jesus' next statement, the paradox:

> For whoever wants to save his life will lose it, but whoever loses his life for me will find it.
>
> —Matthew 16:25

Let me explain it this way. If you hold your life so dear to yourself that you want to use it only to please yourself—to do your own will and follow your own feelings and desires rather than deny self and serve God—*you will actually end up losing your life*. Your life will eventually become hollow and empty. You will get to the end of your life and realize that it was all for nothing—that there was no lasting purpose or meaning to it. But if you choose to lose your life for Jesus' sake by giving up your rights, feelings, desires, and dreams by denying yourself, taking up your cross of sacrifice, and following Christ in everything you do, *you will truly find your life*. Simply put, if you give up and lose your life in sacrifice and service to God, you will actually find your life. That's the paradox!

What happens if you only want to please yourself, do your own thing and follow your own feelings and desires?

_____

_____

_____

What happens if you are willing to give up your rights, your desires, and your dreams for Jesus' sake?

_____

_____

_____

Now, you may have noticed that woven within this paradox is yet another paradox: *you must die to self to live.* Second Corinthians 5:15 states it like this:

And he died for all, that those who live *should no longer live for themselves* but for him who died for them and was raised again (emphasis added).

You are called to no longer live for yourself. In other words, you are called to die to self. The reason? Because you are chosen to bear fruit that will last.

John 12:24 explains it this way:

I tell you the truth, unless a kernel of wheat falls to the ground and dies, it remains only a single seed. But if it dies, it produces many seeds.

A person has to die to bear fruit!

To bear fruit—to live a life that will compel people to want to follow Christ—you have to die to your selfish feelings and desires. You have to die to your so-called rights in order to be a living sacrifice that will bear fruit. Remember, people are watching, and your actions will speak louder than your words. You are called by God to be an example of Christ to the world, for according to God's Word, you have been chosen to bear such fruit.

Let me explain it this way. If I were to die to myself, then there would be no more me, myself or I. I would live 100 percent to please God. I would not sit around licking my wounds and demanding my rights, because I would no longer be chewing the cud. I would immediately give that cud to God and lay down my life (which includes any hurts, feelings, or desires), because my life would no longer be mine! This would keep me from all the cruddy consequence-spitting.

The amazing paradoxes of the Christian life! As you lay down your life, you find it. As you die to self, you live. As you give up things, you receive more in return.

> But seek first his kingdom and his righteousness, and all these things will be given to you as well.
> —Matthew 6:33

It's amazing! As you let go of all the things you thought you wanted, God gives you more. As you let go of your dreams, God gives you back even greater dreams that become reality. If you hold onto everything—mine, mine, mine, me, me, me—you end up with an empty and sad life. But as you give up the things that seem so precious to you, God gives back tenfold. It's a miracle that you will only see unfolding in your life as you willingly live a life of paradox.

Let me share one final story with you. From the time that one of my daughters was about five years old, she wanted to be a nurse. She held on to this dream for years. When she was in high school, she researched all the different colleges that offered programs in nursing. She eventually picked Biola University, a Christian college, because in addition to having a nursing program, the school also had a strong emphasis on missionary work. Unfortunately, Biola University costs over 30,000 dollars a year to attend, and the program takes five years to complete. You do the math. This seemed impossible, because we were missionaries and didn't have a large income. My daughter had dreamed and dreamed of one day attending and graduating from Biola, but now God was calling her to give up her dream. He was calling her to place Him first in her heart.

Is there anything—a right, a dream, a desire—that you are placing before God in your heart?

_____

_____

_____

Remember, you cannot serve two masters. Are you willing to place God first?

_____

_____

_____

Are you willing to lose your life to find it?

_____

_____

_____

God called my daughter to deny herself and take up her cross by sacrificing her dream of attending Biola, choosing to follow Him instead. Although she could have attended a different college in California, she felt God was calling her to return to Bulgaria and do her first year of college via the Internet. As a mom, it was difficult to watch my daughter die to self and live for Christ, because I knew the depth of her dream to attend Biola. It broke my heart that we couldn't afford to send her to that university. If it were within my power, I would have given her this dream.

But God had greater plans. He knew that as my daughter died to self and lived for Him, it would build up her character. She is His work of art. She is His work in progress. He is molding and making her into who He wants her to be. You, too, are His work of art. He desires to build your character and will call you to give up your rights, dreams, and desires so that you can become all that He intends you to be. For you are chosen.

So my daughter stayed in Bulgaria, and God used her mightily that year. Besides studying via the Internet, she also worked with the youth group at the Bulgarian church we attended. God called her to disciple one special young lady who was a new Christian. Every week, they would meet at our house and study the Bible together. I watched as this young lady grew into a young woman who loves the Lord and desires to serve Him. I know without a doubt that God kept my daughter in Bulgaria that year for this young woman. I know that my daughter has rewards in heaven for denying self, for taking up her cross as she sacrificed her dream, and for following Christ.

This young woman has since married. She and her husband attended Bible College in Hungary, and God has been using them in Bulgaria to bear fruit. It is amazing! In John 12:24, Jesus said,

> I tell you the truth, unless a kernel of wheat falls to the ground and dies, it remains only a single seed. But if it dies, it produces many seeds.

God called my daughter to die to self in order to live. As she died to self, she bore fruit. Now, that fruit is multiplying in the young woman's life as she, too, chooses to die to self and live for Christ. It is absolutely amazing to watch how God multiplies the fruit in a person's life.

What is even more amazing is this: because my daughter willingly died to herself and gave up her dreams, she discovered how wonderful it is to serve God. She discovered the joy in sacrificing for Him. As she followed God's Word—"Seek first his kingdom and his righteousness, and all these things will be given to you" (Matthew 6:33)—she found her life. Better yet, God blessed her. He gave her the desires of her heart. The next year, God *provided* for her to attend Biola University. He also miraculously (long story) opened the door for her not only to attend Biola as an undergraduate, but also to get into the nursing program—a program that accepts only 30 students each year!

God will call you to die to self also. He will call you to lose your life. But the paradox is this: the life you find as you give up your own will be so much more amazing than any you could have ever imagined. So I challenge you to lose your life so that you will find it! Die to self so that you will live!

To accomplish this, you must have the attitude of, "It's not about me, it's all about Christ." The pity-party attitude of "life's not fair" or "no one loves me" is no longer acceptable. So what if people aren't nice to you. You be the one who is nice, no matter what. So what if people don't care about you. You be the one who cares for others, no matter what. So what if life isn't fair. You be the one who is fair in every situation. This is what it means to die to self and live for Christ. This is when you will bear fruit. Remember that you are chosen to go and bear fruit—fruit that will last, for you are Christ's ambassador here on earth.

God is looking for the teen who is willing to be humble, gentle, kind, and compassionate, even when he (or she) is being treated unjustly. God is looking for the teen who will be patient and bear with others in love, even those prickly people. God is looking for the teen who loves the unlovable. God is looking for the teen who will walk in integrity and fairness, even when a situation seems unfair. God is looking for the teen who will not compromise, even when everyone else is. God is looking for the teen who will walk in purity, even when everyone else is not. God is looking for the teen who is not ashamed to stand for the truth, even when it is unpopular. God is looking for the teen who will deny self, even when everyone else is living for self. God is looking for the teen who will take up the cross and suffer difficulties and hardships for Him. God is looking for the teen who will follow Him no matter where He calls him (or her) to go or no matter what He calls him (or her) to do. God is looking for the teen who is willing to lose his (or her) life to find His perfect will. As Brian Bell has stated, "The world needs you, Christian, to see your character on display daily which will result in genuine fruit."[11]

God allows trials, temptations, difficult situations, and prickly people to bring you to the place in which you will be required to give up your rights, your feelings, and your desires. He will bring you to the place where you will be required to die to self so that you can become all He intends you to be. He is more concerned about your character than your situation. In Galatians 2:20, Paul explains it this way:

> I have been crucified with Christ. It is no longer I who live, but Christ who lives in me. And the life I now live in the flesh I live by faith in the Son of God, who loved me and gave himself for me.
>
> —ESV

Which choice will you make?

Which choice will you make? Will you make the foolish choice to live by your feelings and desires? Or will you make the wise choice to live by faith in the Son of God, who loves you and gave Himself for you?

There is another interesting paradox:

> But God chose the foolish things of the world to shame
> the wise; God chose the weak things of the world to shame
> the strong.
>
> —1 Corinthians 1:27

Maybe you have made mistakes. Maybe you have lived by your feelings and desires. Maybe you have made foolish choices. It is not too late for you! God uses the foolish things of the world to shame and confound the wise. All that you need to do to get right with God is to admit, confess, and repent of your sin. Remember, the word *repent* means to *change* your ways. If you have been living for self, change your ways and live for God! The key is to rely on God. Get your strength from God.

Hebrews 12:1 encourages us with this:

> Let us throw off everything that hinders and *the sin that so
> easily entangles,* and let us run with perseverance the race
> marked out for us (emphasis added).

James 1:5 declares,

> If you need wisdom—if you want to know what God
> wants you to do—ask him, and he will gladly tell you.
>
> —NLT

So rely on God! Get your strength from Him! As you seek Him, He will give you the wisdom to make wise choices so that your life will not be entangled by sin!

In closing, here is one more important definition of *calling*: "The action of God in summoning people to specific tasks or roles."[12] Besides being called to do everything that we talked about in this chapter, God may call you to a specific task or role. We see specific calls on different peoples' lives throughout the Bible. For instance, Moses was called to set God's people free from Egypt,[13] the prophet Jeremiah was called to go and preach God's warnings to His people,[14] and the apostle Paul was called to preach the gospel to the Gentiles.[15]

I, myself, was called to write this book. I knew without a doubt that the Holy Spirit had placed on my heart a strong inner call to write this book. I also am called to be a missionary in Bulgaria. It is a summons by God that I cannot deny. Believe me, I have tried at times to ignore His summons, but I have discovered in my Christian walk that there is no peace within my heart when I am not following God's call.

You also have a call upon your life. You were created for a specific purpose. But you will only discover your calling and purpose as you live a life of paradox, which is why I am challenging you to live this grand adventure.

If you take the principles you have learned in this book and apply them to your life daily (sometimes moment by moment), you will *go in peace!* You live in a sinful world and, as

Die to self, live for Christ!

a result, you will experience new hurts from time to time. The moment something hurtful happens, remember to *die to self, live for Christ,* and *give it to God.* If you realize that you are continually chewing on something by thinking about it over and over again, remember that is chewing the cud. Stop! *Die to self, live for Christ,* and *give it to God.* If you recognize cruddy consequences in your life, take the time to search your heart and sit down and write a letter again if you need to do so. *Die to self, live for Christ,* and *give it to God.* And as you encounter troublesome situations and trials each day, remember that when you lose your life, you will find it. As you live this life of paradox, it will help keep you from falling into the vicious downward spiral of sin, sin, and more sin, which will allow you to *go in peace!*

Psalm 85:8 warns,

> I will listen to what God the LORD will say; he promises peace to his people, his saints—*but let them not return to folly* (emphasis added).

Do not return to your folly. Apply what you have learned to your life. From the first chapter of this book until now, you learned that you were not a mistake. You were created for a specific purpose. You are God's workmanship created in Christ Jesus to do a good work. Not only that, but you are also called by God. You are an ambassador for Christ. You are called to no longer live for yourself, but to die to self and live for Christ, for you have been chosen to go and bear fruit.

In view of all this, be all that God intends you to be. Live your life worthy of your calling. Serve Him to the best of your ability.

> For God's gifts and his call are irrevocable.
> —Romans 11:29

As you live your life worthy of your calling, you will *go in peace!*

DIGGING DEEPER

In this chapter, you learned many truths of who you are in Christ. Take the time to look up the following verses and underline or highlight them in your Bible. Then write any that are special to you in a journal or on a 3×5 card so that you can memorize them and have them close at hand when you need encouragement. Also listed under the extra credit are verses that support your calling. Remember, God loves you more than you know. I pray that you will walk worthy of your calling. *Go in peace!*

You are called of God—Romans 11:29;
   1 Thessalonians 2:11–12; 2 Timothy 1:8–9;
   1 Peter 5:10–11; 2 Peter 1:10; Jude 1:1
You are chosen—Ephesians 1:4–5; 1 Thessalonians 1:4
You are chosen to go and bear fruit—John 15:16
You are an ambassador for Christ—2 Corinthians 5:20;
   Ephesians 6:19–20
You are called to no longer live for yourself—
   2 Corinthians 5:15
You are called to die to self and live for Christ—
   Matthew 16:24–26; Mark 8:34; Luke 9:23–24
You are to go in peace—Colossians 3:15;
   Luke 7:48 and 50

Extra Credit: Your Calling

Your calling is a worthy call—Ephesians 4:1;
  2 Thessalonians 1:11

You are called to live a holy life—2 Timothy 1:8–9;
  1 Peter 1:15

You are called to stand true to the gospel of grace—
  Galatians 1:6

You are called to fellowship—1 Corinthians 1:9–10

You are called to submit to those whom God has placed
  over you—1 Peter 2:13–21

You are called to treat people with God's love as you
  overcome evil with good and repay insult with
  blessing—Romans 12:21; 1 Peter 3:9

You are called to rely on God for wisdom and power—
  1 Corinthians 1:24

You are called to stand firm in the midst of trials and
  temptations—2 Timothy 1:8–9; 1 Peter 5:10–11

You are called to be free—Galatians 5:13

Your call is an irrevocable call which means that you are
  bound to it and cannot change it—Romans 11:29

Your call is filled with hope—Ephesians 1:18

You are called to step out of the darkness and into His
  wonderful light—1 Peter 2:9

You are called to have peace in your heart—
  Colossians 3:15

Your call is an upward call, a call towards heaven—
  Philippians 3:14; Hebrews 3:1

You are to make your calling sure—2 Peter 1:10

Your calling is not to be taken lightly! *Go in peace!*

CRUDDY CONSEQUENCES

When you choose to chew on the cud of your hurt, pain, anger, and bitterness, instead of giving it to God in the manner He intended, there will be consequences. Listed below are verses about the different consequences that you will suffer. These have been provided to remind you that if you suffer from a particular consequence, *you are not alone.* In addition, because each of these consequences is listed in the Bible, you can also be assured that the answer for how to deal with these consequences can also be discovered in the Bible! So following the verses describing the consequences, you will also find a verse or verses on how to *overcome* the consequence. Jesus said,

> If you hold to my teaching, you are really my disciples. Then you will know the truth, and the truth will set you free.
>
> —John 8:31–32

As you hold to His teaching, you will be set free, which will equip you to *go in peace!*

Guilt

- Psalm 38:4: "My guilt has overwhelmed me like a burden too heavy to bear."
- Psalm 69:5: "You know my folly, O God; my guilt is not hidden from you."
- Jeremiah 2:22: "'Although you wash yourself with soda and use an abundance of soap, the stain of your guilt is still before me,' declares the Sovereign LORD."

To overcome

- Psalm 32:5: "Then I acknowledged my sin to you and did not cover up my iniquity. I said, 'I will confess my transgressions to the LORD'—and you forgave the guilt of my sin."

It is important to be honest with yourself and God. As you are honest, you can then admit, confess, and repent of your sin so that you can *go in peace!*

Shame

- Psalm 44:15: "My disgrace is before me all day long, and my face is covered with shame."
- Psalm 83:16: "Cover their faces with shame so that men will seek your name, O LORD."

To overcome

- Psalm 34:5: "Those who look to him are radiant; their faces are never covered with shame."

God can set you free from the shame if you seek His name and turn to Him. Continue to work through this book and apply what you learn to your life. As you do this, you will discover that you truly can be set free from the shame so that you can *go in peace!*

Fear

- Proverbs 29:25: "Fear of man will prove to be a snare."

To overcome:

- Psalm 56:3–6, 11: "When I am afraid, I will trust in you. In God, whose word I praise, in God I trust; I will not be afraid. What can mortal man do to me? All day long they twist my words; they are always plotting to harm me. They conspire, they lurk, they watch my steps, eager to take my life. . . . In God I trust; I will not be afraid. What can man do to me?"
- Isaiah 43:1–2: "But now, this is what the LORD says—he who created you, O Jacob, he who formed you, O Israel: 'Fear not, for I have redeemed you; I have summoned you by name; you are mine. When you pass through the waters, I will be with you; and when you pass through the rivers, they will not sweep over you. When you walk through the fire, you will not be burned; the flames will not set you ablaze.'"

Instead of being filled with fear, trust in God. Learn the promises of God's Word and apply them to your life so that you can *go in peace!*

Anxiety

- Psalm 38:10: "My heart pounds, my strength fails me; even the light has gone from my eyes."

To overcome:

- Isaiah 26:3–4: "You will keep in perfect peace him whose mind is steadfast, because he trusts in you. Trust in the LORD forever, for the LORD, the LORD, is the Rock eternal."

- Philippians 4:6–7: "Do not be anxious about anything, but in everything, by prayer and petition, with thanksgiving, present your requests to God. And the peace of God, which transcends all understanding, will guard your hearts and your minds in Christ Jesus."

When the anxiety first begins, do not focus on it. Instead, focus on the truth of God and His Word. Do what the verse says: do not be anxious about anything, instead present your requests to God. This is why it is important to memorize verses so that you can change your focus. This is what will equip you to *go in peace!*

Denial and Avoidance

- 1 John 1:6, 8: "If we claim to have fellowship with him yet walk in the darkness, we lie and do not live by

183

the truth. . . . If we claim to be without sin, we deceive ourselves and the truth is not in us."

To overcome:

- 1 John 1:9: "If we confess our sins, he is faithful and just and will forgive us our sins and purify us from all unrighteousness."

Remember to admit, confess, and repent of your sin. When you do this, you have overcome the denial and avoidance and can *go in peace!*

Blame

- Genesis 3:11–13: "And he [God] said, 'Who told you that you were naked? Have you eaten from the tree that I commanded you not to eat from?' The man said, 'The woman you put here with me—she gave me some fruit from the tree, and I ate it.' Then the LORD God said to the woman, 'What is this you have done?' The woman said, 'The serpent deceived me, and I ate.'"

To overcome:

- Proverbs 28:13: "He who conceals his sins does not prosper, but whoever confesses and renounces them finds mercy."

Do not try to conceal your sin by blaming others. Instead, admit, confess, and repent of your sin so that you can *go in peace!*

Bad Memories

- Psalm 13:2: "How long must I wrestle with my thoughts and everyday have sorrow in my heart?"

To overcome:

- Psalm 13:5–6: "But I trust in your unfailing love; my heart rejoices in your salvation. I will sing to the LORD, for he has been good to me."

- Philippians 4:8: "Finally, brothers, whatever is true, whatever is noble, whatever is right, whatever is pure, whatever is lovely, whatever is admirable—if anything is excellent or praiseworthy—think about such things."

When the bad memories come, do not dwell on them, but change your thinking. Think on the things listed in Philippians 4:8. Find something else to dwell on—something true, something noble. As you change your thinking, you will *go in peace!*

Nightmares

- Daniel 4:5: "I had a dream that made me afraid. As I was lying in my bed, the images and visions that passed through my mind terrified me."

- Job 7:13–14: "When I think my bed will comfort me and my couch will ease my complaint, even then you frighten me with dreams and terrify me with visions."

To overcome:

- Psalm 3:5: "I lie down and sleep; I wake again, because the Lord sustains me."
- Psalm 4:8: "I will lie down and sleep in peace, for you alone, O Lord, make me dwell in safety."
- Proverbs 3:24–26: "When you lie down, you will not be afraid; Yes, you will lie down and your sleep will be sweet. Do not be afraid of sudden terror, Nor of trouble from the wicked when it comes; For the Lord will be your confidence, And keep your foot from being caught" (NKJV).

Focus on God and His Word, not on the nightmare. Memorize Psalm 3:5 and 4:8. Then you can repeat these verses to yourself as you are falling back to sleep. As you stay focused on God and His Word, you will sleep *in peace!*

Depression

Many times, depression comes as a result of sin or as a result of grief.

DEPRESSION AS A RESULT OF SIN

- Genesis 4:6–7: "Then the Lord said to Cain, 'Why are you angry? Why is your face downcast? If you do what is right, will you not be accepted? But if you do not do what is right, sin is crouching at your door; it desires to have you, but you must master it.'"
- Psalm 38:1–2, 6 and 8: "O Lord, do not rebuke me in your anger or discipline me in your wrath. For your arrows have pierced me, and your hand has come down upon me. . . . I am bowed down and brought

very low; all day long I go about mourning. . . . I am feeble and utterly crushed; I groan in anguish of heart."

To overcome depression as a result of sin:

- Psalm 32:2–7: "Blessed is the man whose sin the LORD does not count against him and in whose spirit is no deceit. When I kept silent, my bones wasted away through my groaning all day long. For day and night your hand was heavy upon me; my strength was sapped as in the heat of summer. Then I acknowledged my sin to you and did not cover up my iniquity. I said, 'I will confess my transgressions to the LORD'—and you forgave the guilt of my sin. Therefore let everyone who is godly pray to you while you may be found; surely when the mighty waters rise, they will not reach him. You are my hiding place; you will protect me from trouble and surround me with songs of deliverance."

If your depression is a result of sin, acknowledge your sin to yourself and God by admitting, confessing, and repenting of it.

DEPRESSION AS A RESULT OF GRIEF

- Lamentations 3:1–3 and 8: "I am the man who has seen affliction by the rod of his wrath. He has driven me away and made me walk in darkness rather than light; indeed, he has turned his hand against me again and again, all day long. . . . Even when I call out or cry for help, he shuts out my prayer."

To overcome depression as a result of grief:

- Lamentations 3:22–23 and 32: "Because of the LORD's great love we are not consumed, for his compassions never fail. They are new every morning; . . . Though he brings grief, he will show compassion, so great is his unfailing love."

If your depression results from grief, know that even though life is difficult and there are sad situations, you can still avoid depression in the midst of the sad situation by focusing on God and His Word.

To find encouragement:

- 2 Corinthians 4:8–9, 16–18: "We are hard pressed on every side, but not crushed; perplexed, but not in despair; persecuted, but not abandoned; struck down, but not destroyed. . . . Therefore we do not lose heart. Though outwardly we are wasting away, yet inwardly we are being renewed day by day. For our light and momentary troubles are achieving for us an eternal glory that far outweighs them all. So we fix our eyes not on what is seen, but on what is unseen. For what is seen is temporary, but what is unseen is eternal."

It is important to live according to God's Word, not according to your feelings. Ask God for the strength to get out of bed everyday. Then take the next step by rolling over and getting up. As you do, you will discover that God meets you there. He will give you the strength to make it through the day, but you have to take the first two steps by asking God to give you the strength and by rolling over and getting out of bed. As you do, you will *go in peace!*

Rage or Anger

- Genesis 4:6 and 8: "'Why are you so angry?' the Lord asked him [Cain]. 'Why do you look so dejected?' . . . Later Cain suggested to his brother, Abel, 'Let's go out into the fields.' And while they were there, Cain attacked and killed his brother" (NLT).

- Ephesians 4:26–27: "'In your anger do not sin:' Do not let the sun go down while you are still angry, and do not give the devil a foothold."

To overcome:

- Genesis 4:7: "You will be accepted if you respond in the right way. But if you refuse to respond correctly, then watch out! Sin is waiting to attack and destroy you, and you must subdue it" (NLT).

God warned Cain to respond the right way, according to His Word. And God warned Cain that if he did not watch out, sin was waiting to destroy him. Therefore, God warned Cain to subdue the sin that was in his heart.

- Psalm 4:4–5: "In your anger do not sin; when you are on your beds, search your hearts and be silent. Offer right sacrifices and trust in the LORD."

- Psalm 139:23–24: "Search me, O God, and know my heart; test me and know my anxious thoughts. See if there is any offensive way in me, and lead me in the way everlasting."

It is important to take your hurt, pain, anger, and bitterness, and give it to God in the manner He intended. Do not stuff it deep down inside, where it will become infected! Instead, be willing to be honest with yourself. Search your heart and offer any offensive way to the Lord once and for all. As you do this, you will *go in peace!*

Overprotectiveness

- Psalm 38:12: "Those who seek my life set their traps, those who would harm me talk of my ruin; all day long they plot deception."

- Psalm 55:4–5, 8: "My heart is in anguish within me; the terrors of death assail me. Fear and trembling have beset me; horror has overwhelmed me. . . . I would hurry to my place of shelter, far from the tempest and the storm."

To overcome:

- Psalm 32:7: "You are my hiding place; you will protect me from trouble and surround me with songs of deliverance."

- Proverbs 18:10: "The name of the LORD is a strong tower; the righteous run to it and are safe."

When you are fearful for yourself or a loved one, remember to turn to God. He is your Protector. Ask Him to hide you or your loved one in the shadow of His wings. He will be faithful, for He loves you more than you know. As you run to Him, you will *go in peace!*

Appendix 1: Cruddy Consequences

Relationship Difficulties

- Psalm 31:11–12: "I am a dread to my friends—those who see me on the street flee from me. I am forgotten by them as though I were dead: I have become like broken pottery."

- Psalm 38:11: "My friends and companions avoid me because of my wounds; my neighbors stay far away."

To overcome:

- Colossians 3:13–14: "Bear with each other and forgive whatever grievances you may have against one another. Forgive as the Lord forgave you. And over all these virtues put on love, which binds them all together in perfect unity."

- Psalm 31:7, 14: "I will be glad and rejoice in your love, for you saw my affliction and knew the anguish of my soul. . . . but I trust in you, O LORD; I say, 'You are my God.'"

- Ephesians 4:29: "Don't use foul or abusive language. Let everything you say be good and helpful, so that your words will be an encouragement to those who hear them" (NLT).

When you find yourself spitting cruddy consequences on everyone around you, which is causing them to want to avoid you, *stop*! Read chapter 4 of this book and get rid of the infection within your heart, so that people will no longer want to avoid you. Also, if you see that you have built a protective wall around yourself which is keeping you from making any friends, *stop*! Again, read chapter 4 and get rid of the infection within your heart. Take a chance at making friends. Look for someone who has a strong relationship with the Lord. In other words, look for someone who will help pull you up into heaven, not someone who will pull you down into the gutter. Finding a friend who is trying to become more and more like Jesus is usually someone who will not intentionally hurt you.

Self-Destructive Behaviors

ANOREXIA

- 2 Samuel 12:16–17: "David pleaded with God for the child. He fasted and went into his house and spent the nights lying on the ground. The elders of his household stood beside him to get him up from the ground, but he refused, and he would not eat any food with them."

People become anorexic for many different reasons. For some, it is a focus on their body. They do not want to become fat, and their body becomes their idol. For others, anorexia is a way of seeking attention. And for many, anorexia is a way of seeking control.

To overcome anorexia as a result of self-focus:

- 1 Corinthians 3:16–17: "Don't you know that you yourselves are God's temple and that God's Spirit lives in you? If anyone destroys God's temple, God will destroy him; for God's temple is sacred, and you are that temple."

- 1 Corinthians 6:19–20: "Do you not know that your body is a temple of the Holy Spirit, who is in you, whom you have received from God? You are not your own; you were bought at a price. Therefore honor God with your body."

- 2 Corinthians 6:16: "What agreement is there between the temple of God and idols? For we are the
  temple of the living God."

- 2 Corinthians 6:14: "For what do righteousness and
  wickedness have in common? Or what fellowship can
  light have with darkness?"

If you struggle with anorexia because you have become too
focused on your weight, it is important to realize that this
behavior is sin. You are neglecting to care for your body in
the manner which God intended.[1] Your body has become
your idol. You are "worshipping thinness and making [your]
appearance and weight an idol."[2]

To overcome anorexia as a result of seeking attention:

- Luke 9:23: "Then he [Jesus] said to them all: 'If anyone would come after me, he must deny himself and
  take up his cross daily and follow me.'"

If you are using anorexia as a means of seeking attention,
you need to realize that this also is sin, because you are focused
on self and not on God.[3]

To overcome anorexia as a result of seeking control:

- 2 Samuel 12:16–17: "David pleaded with God for
  the child. He fasted and went into his house and
  spent the nights lying on the ground. The elders of
  his household stood beside him to get him up from
  the ground, but he refused, and he would not eat any
  food with them."

- 2 Samuel 12:20: "Then David got up from the ground. After he had washed, put on lotions and changed his clothes, he went into the house of the LORD and worshiped. Then he went to his own house, and at his request they served him food, and he ate."

For many, anorexia is a means of seeking control.[4] Sometimes, when a person is grieving or has experienced a deep hurt, they just don't feel like eating. This is normal. However, it becomes a problem when this behavior continues for more than a few days. Soon, not eating becomes comfortable and something that is controllable in a world that seems out of control. The person is attempting to be in control instead of submitting to God, which is also a sin.

King David was grieving the sickness of his child. In his case, he was seeking God in a godly manner as he fasted and prayed for the Lord to intercede on his child's behalf, because he did not allow his fasting to continue for too long. If you are struggling with anorexia because you have used it as a means of control, you need to be like King David. Get up, worship the Lord no matter what is going on around you or how you are feeling, and develop healthy eating habits!

You can read the entire story about King David's sin, which led to a deep heart hurt when his child died, and how he overcame it, in 2 Samuel chapters 11–12. You can also re-read chapter 9 of this book, where you learned how to overcome by denying self so that you can *go in peace!*

BULIMIA
- Proverbs 28:7: "He who keeps the law is a discerning son, but a companion of gluttons disgraces his father."

- Proverbs 23:21: "For drunkards and gluttons become poor, and drowsiness clothes them in rags."

To overcome:

- Proverbs 23:19–21: "Listen, my son, and be wise, and keep your heart on the right path. Do not join those who drink too much wine or gorge themselves on meat, for drunkards and gluttons become poor, and drowsiness clothes them in rags."
- Philippians 4:13: "I can do everything through him [Christ] who gives me strength."

A *glutton* is a person who overeats. For the person suffering with bulimia "eating has become her god. [However,] God wants her to hunger and thirst for Him. She must replace the desire to eat with a desire to find abundant satisfaction in God. She needs an understanding of God's holiness and His hatred of sin. She must see her eating as idolatry and understand that she is in bondage to her sin."[5]

As with anorexia, if you are struggling with bulimia, you need to remember that your body is a dwelling place for God's Holy Spirit and that you are commanded to care for it. Rely on God to give you the strength to overcome your unhealthy eating habits. There is nothing too hard for Him. As you rely on God, you will *go in peace!*

DRUGS AND ALCOHOL

- Proverbs 20:1: "Wine is a mocker, strong drink a brawler, and whoever is led astray by it is not wise" (ESV).

- Luke 21:34: "Be careful, or your hearts will be weighed down with dissipation, drunkenness and the anxieties of life, and that day will close on you unexpectedly like a trap."

- Proverbs 23:29–35: "Who has woe? Who has sorrow? Who has strife? Who has complaints? Who has needless bruises? Who has bloodshot eyes? Those who linger over wine, who go to sample bowls of mixed wine. Do not gaze at wine when it is red, when it sparkles in the cup, when it goes down smoothly! In the end it bites like a snake and poisons like a viper. Your eyes will see strange sights and your mind imagine confusing things. You will be like one sleeping on the high seas, lying on top of the rigging. 'They hit me,' you will say, 'but I'm not hurt! They beat me, but I don't feel it! When will I wake up so I can find another drink?'"

To overcome:

- Ephesians 5:15–18: "Be very careful, then, how you live—not as unwise but as wise, making the most of every opportunity, because the days are evil. Therefore do not be foolish, but understand what the Lord's will is. Do not get drunk on wine, which leads to debauchery. Instead, be filled with the Spirit."

- 1 Corinthians 5:11: "But now I am writing you that you must not associate with anyone who calls himself a brother but is sexually immoral or greedy, an idolater or a slanderer, a drunkard or a swindler. With such a man do not even eat."

- 1 Corinthians 6:9–11: "Do you not know that the wicked will not inherit the kingdom of God? Do not be deceived: Neither the sexually immoral nor idolaters nor adulterers nor male prostitutes nor homosexual offenders nor thieves nor the greedy *nor drunkards* nor slanderers nor swindlers will inherit the kingdom of God. *And that is what some of you were.* But you were washed, you were sanctified, you were justified in the name of the Lord Jesus Christ and by the Spirit of our God" (emphasis added).

- Philippians 4:13: "I can do everything through him [Christ] who gives me strength."

- Psalm 105:4: "Look to the LORD and his strength; seek his face always."

God's Word tells you not to get drunk on wine and not to associate with those who do, those who might influence you to go down that same path. If you are struggling with drugs or alcohol, understand that it is possible for you to be set free (see chapter 8 for more encouragement on this). However, you must look to the Lord for His strength to live your life according to His Word. As you do, you will *go in peace!*

CUTTING

- Deuteronomy 14:1–2: "You are children of the LORD your God. Do not cut yourselves or shave the front of your heads for the dead, for you are a people holy to the LORD your God. Out of all the peoples on the face of the earth, the LORD has chosen you to be his treasured possession."

- Leviticus 19:28: "Do not cut your bodies for the dead or put tattoo marks on yourselves. I am the LORD."

- Mark 5:5: "Night and day among the tombs and in the hills he would cry out and cut himself with stones."

To overcome:

- Psalm 73:21–28: "When my heart was grieved and my spirit embittered, I was senseless and ignorant . . . Yet I am always with you; you hold me by my right hand. You guide me with your counsel . . . My flesh and my heart may fail, but God is the strength of my heart and my portion forever. Those who are far from you will perish; you destroy all who are unfaithful to you. But as for me, it is good to be near God. I have made the Sovereign LORD my refuge; I will tell of all your deeds."

Sometimes, people can hurt so badly that they erect a protective barrier around themselves which causes them to get to the place of complete numbness. For them, cutting can be a way to feel something—anything—again. For others, cutting is a means of punishment that they feel they deserve. And for some, it is a means for attention. They are crying out for someone to help heal their broken heart. If you struggle with cutting, you need to take the focus off of the hurt, anger, and bitterness you are feeling. In other words, stop the pity party! If you only focus on your hurt, anger, and bitterness, God's Word says that you are senseless and ignorant. You are missing all that God has for you. Instead, do what God's Word says: Admit your sin to yourself, confess it to God, and repent. As you do these three things, realize that God is with you, whether you feel that He is or not. Allow Him to guide you with the counsel of His Word. Allow Him to be your strength every day. Draw near to God, for this is good. Make Him your refuge so that you will *go in peace!*

Appendix 1: Cruddy Consequences

SUICIDAL THOUGHTS AND/OR ATTEMPTS

- Job 3:11, 16, 20–22: "Why did I not perish at birth, and die as I came from the womb? . . . Or why was I not hidden in the ground like a stillborn child, like an infant who never saw the light of day? . . . Why is light given to those in misery, and life to the bitter of soul, to those who long for death that does not come, who search for it more than for hidden treasure, who are filled with gladness and rejoice when they reach the grave."

To overcome:

- Jeremiah 29:11–14: "'For I know the plans I have for you,' declares the LORD, 'plans to prosper you and not to harm you, plans to give you hope and a future. Then you will call upon me and come and pray to me, and I will listen to you. You will seek me and find me when you seek me with all your heart. I will be found by you,' declares the LORD, 'and will bring you back from captivity.'"

Suicide is a permanent answer to a temporary problem. Everyone has problems at some time or other, but these problems and even sad feelings can be solved. If you truly wish to die, then die the biblical way. If you die the biblical way—die to yourself and live for Christ—you will discover that your suicidal thoughts will disappear (see chapter 9 for more about dying to self). Second Corinthians 5:15 states it this way:

> And he died for all, that those who live *should no longer live for themselves* but for him who died for them and was raised again. You are called to no longer live for yourself but for Christ who died for you (emphasis added).

So die to self, get the focus off of your problems, and turn to God. Ask Him to show you His plan for your life, and then get up and go help someone else. Live for Christ! As you do, you will *go in peace!*

Conclusion

- Ezra 9:13–14: "What has happened to us is a result of our evil deeds and our great guilt, and yet, our God, you have punished us less than our sins have deserved . . . Shall we again break your commands and intermarry with the peoples who commit such detestable practices? Would you not be angry enough with us to destroy us, leaving us no remnant or survivor?"

In the verses above, the Israelites were considering sinning more than they had already, so that God would be so angry that He would zap them and destroy them. Don't be like the Israelites. Don't choose to punish yourself more than God's loving discipline would have warranted. God truly does punish us less than our sins deserve. He is slow to anger. He is gracious and He loves us deeply.

We are crazy people! We do all kinds of crazy things to ourselves as a means of punishment. We are unable to forgive ourselves. We choose bad relationships. We hurt good relationships. We become anorexic or bulimic. We hurt ourselves physically by cutting or some other self-mutilating action. We consider suicide and may even attempt it, all as a means of punishing ourselves, when what we simply need to do is accept God's gift of love, grace, and forgiveness.

Lamentations: 3:19–23 states,

I remember my affliction and my wandering, the bitterness and the gall. I well remember them, and my soul is downcast within me. *Yet this I call to mind and therefore I have hope:* Because of the LORD's great love we are not consumed, for his compassions never fail. They are new every morning; great is your faithfulness (emphasis added).

So accept His gift! *Go in peace!*

ANSWERS TO QUESTIONS

Chapter 1: You Are Loved

1. According to Jeremiah 31:3, what has God drawn you with?
   Loving kindness.

2. According to this verse, how has He loved you?
   With an everlasting love.

3. Based on what you read in this verse, are you loved by God? Tell the truth. Don't write down what you *feel* but what the *truth* of God's Word says.
   Yes.

4. Write the truth that you are loved.
   I am loved.

5. What are some of the self-inflicted sins which have caused you pain?
   Personal answer. There is no right or wrong response. Answers can include but are not limited to: bad decisions, wrong choices, lying, stealing, rebellion, using alcohol or drugs, sexual immorality, pregnancy outside of marriage, abortion, cutting, eating disorders—the list is endless.

6. What are some of the sins inflicted by another which have caused you hurt?
   Personal answer. There is no right or wrong response. Answers can include but are not limited to: gossip, rejection, mean pranks, abuse (verbal, physical, sexual), rape, incest, parents' divorce, absence of father or mother—the list is endless.

7. According to Romans 3:23, how many people are sinners?
   All.

8. Does that include you and me?
   Yes.

9. Would you agree with the statement that you are a sinner? Why or why not?
   (I pray that your answer was yes! If not, read Romans 3:23 again and write why you think that you are not included in the word "all.")

10. What is included in this big wad of cud?
    Anger and bitterness (Other possible answer: Hurt, pain, anger, and bitterness)

11. Why does God consider this sin?
    Because we do not handle it in the way that God intended.

Chapter 2: Missing the Mark

1. What was the one rule that Adam and Eve were to follow?
   They were not to eat from the tree of knowledge of good and evil.

2. What would happen if they did not follow God's command?
   They would surely die.

3. According to Romans 5:12, when Adam sinned what happened to the entire human race?
   Sin entered the entire human race. (Other possible answers include: Adam's sin brought death; death spread to everyone; everyone sinned.)

4. Does that include you?
   Yes!

5. Has your faith saved you? Have you been born again?
   (Personal answer—no right or wrong response.)

6. If so, when did you become born again? How did it happen?
   (Personal answer—no right or wrong response.)

7. If not, do you want to accept Jesus Christ as your Lord and Savior right now?
   (Personal answer—no right or wrong response. But your response does have eternal consequences so think wisely!)

8. What is wickedness called in human beings?
   Sin

9. Is wickedness or sin of God?
   No!

10. Who was kicked out of heaven?
    Satan (other possible answers include any of Satan's other names such as the devil, the great dragon, the ancient serpent, or Lucifer, to name just a few).

11. Where was he hurled?
    Earth!

12. Who was with him?
    His angels—also known as fallen angels or demons.

Chapter 3: Do Not Be Deceived

1. What is your folly? What are some of the things you have done which have caused you to feel guilt?
    (Personal answer—no right or wrong response.)

2. What are some of the things that have caused you shame?
    (Personal answer—no right or wrong response.)

3. When did sin enter Adam and Eve's lives?
    When they ate the fruit.

4. What made this a sin?
    Because they chose to disobey the one rule that God had given them. (Genesis 2:17: But you must not eat from the tree of the knowledge of good and evil, for when you eat of it you will surely die).

5. What cruddy consequences did Adam and Eve immediately experience?
    Fear, anxiety, avoidance, and denial.

6. Have you ever experienced fear, anxiety, avoidance, and/or denial?
    (Personal answer—no right or wrong response.)

7. If so, which ones?
   (Personal answer—no right or wrong response.)

8. Do you ever try to blame others for your actions?
   (Personal answer—no right or wrong response.)

9. When you blame others, does God consider this sin?
   Yes!

10. Can you get away with your sin, or will God find you out?
    God will find you out!

11. Have you struggled with bad memories, nightmares, or depression?
    (Personal answer—no right or wrong response.)

12. If so, which ones?
    (Personal answer—no right or wrong response.)

13. Is rage, over-protectiveness, relationship difficulties, or self-destructive behavior (such as anorexia, bulimia, cutting or harming yourself, drugs, alcohol, or suicidal thoughts) a part of your life?
    (Personal answer—no right or wrong response.)

14. If so, which ones?
    (Personal answer—no right or wrong response.)

14. Are you like a camel? Which cruddy consequences do you throw up and spit on others? Circle any of the following cruddy consequences that are in your life.
    (Personal answer—no right or wrong response. Circle those that apply to you.)

15. Do you want to be washed clean from all the cruddy consequences?
    (Personal answer—no right or wrong response. But I pray that you said yes!)

Chapter 4: Forgiven and Set Free

1. What separates us from God?
   Our sin of cud-chewing and cruddy-consequence spitting.

2. Why?
   Because we didn't give everything to God in the manner He intended. "Everything" includes the element of deception.

3. Now read Isaiah 59:3–4 again. What do you think these verses mean?
   (Answer varies, but will be something like this: "For your hands are stained with blood, your fingers with guilt" represents our sinful actions. "Your lips have spoken lies, and your tongue mutters wicked things" represents our sinful words. "No one calls for justice; no one pleads his case with integrity" represents our replaying the event in our mind and changing the facts of what really happened as we continue to chew the cud. "They rely on empty arguments and speak lies" represents our sin as we try to deceive ourselves into believing our own lies of making ourselves appear good.)

4. Do you think these verses apply to you?
   Yes! They apply to each and every one of us!

5. Have you done any of these things when you chew on your cud?
   (Answer varies, but hopefully you answered yes and admitted your sin. If you said no, you had best read and memorize 1 John 1:8 and explain why this verse does not apply to you.)

6. Is there someone you are angry with?
   (Personal answer—a word of encouragement: Be honest with yourself. It will set you free.)

7. Are there any others? Be honest, and list everyone with whom you are angry.
   (Personal answer—no right or wrong response.)

8. What do you think these verses mean?
   (Answer varies, but will be something like this: We are not to hold onto our anger. We are not to go to sleep while we are angry. We are to get rid of our anger so it doesn't destroy us.)

9. Have you allowed the sun to go down on your anger? Have you gone to bed while you were still angry?
   (Personal answer, but probably yes. If your answer is no, make sure there is no element of deception within your heart.)

10. What are you to take captive?
    Your thoughts, including all of the hurt, pain, and anger. Plus, don't forget any element of deception.

11. Once taken captive, what are you to do with it?
    Make it obedient to Christ by giving it to Him once and for all. Leave it at His feet like the sinful woman did.

Chapter 5: Forgiveness Is Not an Option

1. What are we to get rid of?
   All bitterness, rage, and anger.

2. Are you ready to get rid of it?
   (Personal answer, but I pray that it is yes!)

3. From the list above do you understand the seven things that *forgiveness is*?
   (Personal answer. However, if your answer is no, ask God to give you wisdom and understanding. Then, slowly reread each paragraph about what forgiveness is that relates to

which portion you don't understand. Take time to think about what you read and again ask God for wisdom and understanding. He will be faithful to answer. As James 1:5 declares, "If you need wisdom—if you want to know what God wants you to do—ask him, and he will gladly tell you. He will not resent your asking" (NLT). Make sure you are being honest with yourself as you do this and that there is no element of deception within you, as many times we like to hold onto our unforgiveness, which makes it easier for us to say we don't understand when really we are just being disobedient to God.)

4. If not, which do you not understand?
   (Personal answer—no right or wrong response.)

5. From the above list, do you understand the seven things that forgiveness is *not*?
   (Personal answer. However, if your answer is no, follow the same steps that are listed in question 3 above.)

6. If not, which do you not understand?
   (Personal answer—no right or wrong response.)

7. Because forgiveness is not an option, are you ready to let go of any bitterness and unforgiveness that you are holding once and for all? Do you want to get rid of this bitterness and unforgiveness completely?
   (Personal answer, but I pray that your answer is yes!)

Chapter 6: Set Apart

1. What three parts did the Tabernacle have?
   The outer court, the Holy Place, and the Holy of Holies.

2. Where did God dwell?
   The Holy of Holies

3. Describe Outer Court Christians. Are they saved? Have they accepted Jesus Christ as their Savior?
   They are saved, but that's it.

4. Are they becoming all who God wants them to be?
   No!

5. Does the Outer Court Christian's life have purpose and meaning or lasting peace and contentment?
   No!

6. Do you desire to be an Outer Court Christian? Or do you want more in your relationship with God? Why?
   (Personal answer, but I pray you do not desire to be an Outer Court Christian and that you want more in your relationship with God!)

7. Describe Holy Place Christians. Are Holy Place Christians living by the truth of God's Word or by their feelings and desires?
   They are living by their feelings and desires, not by the truth of God's Word.

8. What important aspect of their relationship with God is still missing?
   Intimacy!

9. Because this intimacy with God is still missing, have Holy Place Christians found purpose and meaning or lasting peace and contentment in their lives?
   No!

10. Do you desire to be a Holy Place Christian? Or do you want more in your relationship with God? Why or why not?
    (Personal answer, but I pray that you do not desire to be a Holy Place Christian and that you want more in your relationship with God!)

11. When the veil was torn in two from top to bottom, what did this prove?

    It proved that God desires a deep, personal and intimate relationship with us.

12. Does God desire to have an intimate and personal relationship with you?

    Yes!

13. Describe the Holy of Holies Christian. Does the Holy of Holies Christian desire to be all that God intends him or her to be?

    Yes!

14. Is the Holy of Holies Christian constantly aware that sin breaks intimacy with God?

    Yes! The Holy of Holies Christian realizes that sin breaks fellowship with God. Therefore, he or she is continually aware of the sin in his or her own heart.

15. How is intimacy with God restored?

    By taking immediate action to admit, confess, and repent of your sin so that your intimate relationship with God is restored.

16. Is the Holy of Holies Christian's life filled with purpose, meaning, lasting peace, and contentment?

    Yes!

17. Which are you?

    (Personal answer—no right or wrong response.)

18. Is this where you desire to be?

    (Personal answer—no right or wrong response.)

19. If not, what can you do to become a Holy of Holies Christian?

    (Answer varies, but it will be something like this: Read God's Word; pray and spend time seeking God's will daily. He wants to be involved in every aspect of your life, so spend time in His presence and seek His will daily. Also, be aware of the sin in your own heart and immediately admit it to yourself, confess it to God, and repent of it so that your intimate relationship with God is restored.)

Chapter 7: Walk Worthy

1. What does the belt of truth represent?
    The Word of God.

2. What aspect of your life must the Word of God fully encircle?
    Every aspect of your life. (Having every aspect of your life fully encircled by the Word of God means that you make wise choices based on God's Word.)

3. Do you have any examples from your life where you based a decision you made on God's Word?
    (Personal answer, but if you can't think of any, it's not too late to change! Begin today to make wise choices based on the Word of God.)

4. What does the breastplate of righteousness guard?
    Your heart.

5. When do you have the breastplate of righteousness on?
    When you choose to believe in your heart who you are in Christ and make wise decisions based on this truth.

6. Do you know that you are loved, forgiven, victorious, and able to walk worthy of your calling?
   (Personal answer, but I pray that your answer is yes!)

7. Do you believe, in your heart, the truth of who you are in Christ?
   (Personal answer, but again I pray that you answered yes!)

8. What do you prepare the way for as you shod your feet with the preparation of the gospel of peace?
   For others to come to know Christ.

9. What speaks louder than words?
   Our actions.

10. What quenches Satan's fiery darts?
    Faith in God and His Word!

11. What does faith in God and His Word give to you?
    It gives you the strength to walk worthy of your calling.

12. How do you use the shield of faith effectively?
    By deciding in faith to have your mind steadfast on Him and His promises.

13. What does the helmet of salvation protect?
    The mind.

14. What can your thoughts trigger?
    Your actions.

15. What can you do to protect your thought life?
    Change your thinking! As you do, you will be wearing your helmet of salvation.

16. What does the sword of the Spirit represent?
    The Word of God.

17. How do you hide God's Word in your heart so that you are prepared to use the sword of the Spirit?
By reading God's Word and taking the time to memorize verses.

18. Have you allowed the mighty weapon of prayer to rust?
(Personal answer—no right or wrong response.)

19. What does it mean to pray without ceasing?
That you pray always and about everything.

20. What can you receive through prayer?
God's strength, guidance, and wisdom for every situation, trial, and temptation in life.

Chapter 8: Hope and a Future

1. What are the five things that God asks of you in the above passage?
(1) To fear the Lord your God; (2) To walk in all His ways; (3) To love Him; (4) To serve the Lord with all your heart and with all your soul; (5) To observe the Lord's commands and decrees.

2. According to the above passage, why does God ask this of you?
For your own good!

3. According to this passage in Psalms, how can a young person keep his or her way pure? What are the four things listed in the passage?
(1) Live according to God's Word; (2) Seek God with all your heart; (3) Don't stray from God's commands; (4) Hide God's Word in your heart so that you do not sin against God.

4. After looking at these seven practical ways to walk worthy of your calling, are there any that you need to improve on? If so, which ones?
    (Personal answer—no right or wrong response.)

5. What can you do to improve in these areas?
    (Personal answer, but some possible ways include: Read God's Word and live according to it. Change some friends [get rid of any friends who cause you to stumble and fall and find friends who have the same morals and values that you have]. Don't do drugs or drink alcohol. Do not date unbelievers [only date someone who has the same desire toward God that you do—if you desire to be a Holy of Holies Christian, don't date an Outer Court Christian]. Avoid any situation where temptation may occur, such as at the movies or when reading magazines, books or on the Internet [you know what makes you stumble. Whatever that is, avoid it! Do not conform to the patterns of this world. Do not be like everyone else. Stand apart. Pray!])

Chapter 9: You Are Chosen

1. In reviewing your goals, did God work in your life? If so, how?
    (Personal answer—no right or wrong response.)

2. Were most of your goals answered?
    (Personal answer, but I pray they were!)

3. Were you surprised?
    (Personal answer—no right or wrong response.)

4. What are the two meanings of "*called*"?
    (1) A summons or invitation; (2) A strong inner urge or prompting.

5. Do you have a prickly person in your life? Do you have someone who is hard to get along with or difficult to love? If so, who?
   (Personal answer—no right or wrong response.)

6. What is it about that person that makes it so hard to get along with him or her?
   (Personal answer—no right or wrong response.)

7. What are the three principles that Jesus calls us to live by?
   (1) Deny self; (2) Take up your cross; (3) Follow Him.

8. Have you been in a situation recently in which you had to deal with a prickly person?
   (Personal answer—no right or wrong response.)

9. What happened? Did you live by your feelings and desires, or did you deny self, take up your cross and follow Christ?
   (Personal answer. Remember, it is important to be honest with yourself. It is only by being honest with yourself that you can grow and mature into the person God wants you to be.)

10. If you lived by your feelings and desires, what could you have done differently to be an imitator of Christ?
    (Personal answer, but it should be something along the lines of denying self, taking up your cross, and following Christ. The golden rule is to treat others as you yourself would like to be treated.)

11. What happens if you only want to please yourself, do your own thing and follow your own feelings and desires?
    You will actually end up losing your life. Eventually, your life will be hollow and empty. You will get to the end of your life

and realize that it has been for nothing. There is no lasting purpose and meaning.

12. What happens if you are willing to give up your rights, your desires, and your dreams for Jesus' sake?
    You will truly find your life. Your life will have purpose and meaning.

13. Is there anything—a right, a dream, a desire—that you are placing before God in your heart?
    (Personal answer. Be honest!)

14. Remember, you cannot serve two masters. Are you willing to place God first?
    (Personal answer, but I pray your answer is yes!)

15. Are you willing to lose your life to find it?
    (Personal answer, but again, it is my prayer that you said yes!)

APPENDIX 3

PROFILE OF AN ABUSER

Then Asa was angry with the seer [the Lord's prophet
Hanani] and put him in the stocks in prison, for he was in
a rage with him because of this. And Asa inflicted cruelties
upon some of the people at the same time.
—2 Chronicles 16:10 ESV

Unfortunately, because of people's sinful behavior, there
will be those, both male and female, who will not control
their anger and rage and, as a result, will inflict their cruelties
on those around them. The issue of abuse is so prevalent in
society today that you must know what to look for so you
do not end up in an abusive relationship. Abuse is not only
physical, such as hitting or slapping, but it can also be verbal
or sexual. By knowing what to look for at the beginning of
a relationship, you can get out before it is too late. And for
those of you who may already be in an abusive relationship,
know that there is help. Get out before the relationship goes
any longer, especially before you bring babies into it.

218

The profile you are about to read has been compiled from many different sources.[1] Although some of the profiles varied somewhat, I have listed only those traits which were repeated continually. If you would like more information, do an Internet search on the words *profile of an abuser.* You can also visit the web site www.thesheepfold.org, which is a ministry providing help to abuse victims.

If after reading this profile you believe that you are in an abusive relationship, get help! God loves you more than you know, and He does not want you to remain in such a relationship!

Character Traits

CHARISMATIC, ROMANTIC, DEVOTED, AND PROTECTIVE

Is the person charming in public, but degrades you in private? Beware! An abuser is often "charismatic, romantic, devoted and protective. Everyone likes him. On the surface he seems great, so you accept a date with him. He is wonderful. After a few months, you start to notice things but you dismiss them."[2]

JEALOUS AND POSSESSIVE

Is the person possessive and jealous? Be careful! Many abusers are often so jealous they could be described as paranoid. They often have trouble trusting people, especially you. They may continually tell you to "tell the truth" even when you are not lying. Yet, they would describe their possessiveness of you as love.

CONTROLLING

Is the person controlling? Watch out! An abuser likes to be in control at all times. And he likes things his way. He may keep you somewhere against your will or even take away your cell phone. He continually wants to know where you are, who you are with, and what you are doing.

MANIPULATIVE

Is the person manipulative? Take heed! An abuser will, often times, tell you that he cannot live without you. Or that he would die if you left the relationship. He may talk about hurting or killing himself as a means of keeping you in the relationship. Or he may even threaten to harm or kill you if you leave.

DENIES WRONGDOING OR BLAMES OTHERS FOR WRONGFUL BEHAVIOR

Is the person always blaming someone or something else for their own actions? Or do they act as if nothing happened after a terrible rage? Think twice! An abuser will deny their wrongdoing or blame others and situations for what caused the outburst. Often times, the person will even say that it is your fault.

OTHER BEHAVIORAL TRAITS

Does the person tease and say things that hurt? Or force you to have sex? Get out! Many times an abuser has an aggressive attitude. Often times, he will try to make others appear less significant than he feels by putting a person down in front of other people. And he may even be so aggressive that he forces you to have sex with him against your will.

Do friends and family members say this person is not good for you? Listen to what friends and family are saying. Sometimes others will see a situation more clearly than you will when you are "in love." The saying "love is blind" is often true. In addition, it is important to remember who you are in

Christ. You are the child of the King of kings. God does not want you in an abusive relationship. He has plans to give you a hope and a future.

If you answered yes to many of these questions, please get out of the relationship immediately! If you need to go visit a friend or relative away from home for a while, do it! Get away and get help! There are also shelters and other resources available for abuse victims. Do not allow yourself to be manipulated back into the relationship. Rely on God to be your shield. Ask Him to protect you as you take the steps to protect yourself.

> "The Lord is my rock, my fortress, and my savior; my God is my rock, in whom I find protection. He is my shield, the strength of my salvation, and my stronghold, my high tower, my savior, the one who saves me from violence."
> —2 Samuel 22:2–3 NLT

NOTES

How to Use this Book

1. "ponder," *Dictionary.com Unabridged, v 1.1* (New York: Random House, Inc., 2007). http://dictionary.reference.com/browse/ponder.

Chapter 1: You Are Loved

1. "cud," *Merriam-Webster Dictionary* (Springfield, MA: Merriam-Webster, Inc., 2004), p. 174.
2. Donna M. Amaral-Phillips, "Why Do Cattle Chew Their Cud?" University of Kentucky, September 2, 2007. http://www.uky.edu/AG/AnimalSciences/dairy/extension/nut00014/pdf.
3. "crud," *WordNet® 3.0* (Princeton, NJ: Princeton University, 2007). http://dictionary.reference.com/browse/crud.
4. "consequence," *Dictionary.com Unabridged, v 1.1* (New York: Random House, Inc., 2007). http://dictionary.reference.com/browse/consequence.

Chapter 2: Missing the Mark

1. "flesh," *Vine's Complete Expository Dictionary* (Nashville, TN: Thomas Nelson, Inc., 1996), p. 242.
2. See Genesis 5:3.
3. See Romans 7:23.
4. See Ephesians 2:1–2.
5. See Luke 4:5–6; 2 Corinthians 4:4; Colossians 1:13; 1 John 5:19.
6. See Romans 6:6.
7. See Hebrews 9:27.
8. See Revelation 20:15. Part of the preceding paragraph was adapted from *The New Me* Discipleship Curriculum (San Bernardino, CA: Pacific Youth Correctional Ministries, 2003), p. 31.
9. "Jesus," *The NIV Study Bible* (Grand Rapids, MI: Zondervan Bible Publishers, 1985), footnote on p. 1442.
10. "Christ," *The NIV Study Bible*, footnote on p. 1441.
11. See John 1:1,14.
12. See John 10:30.
13. See Deuteronomy 6:4.
14. See Luke 24:49; John 14:16–17; Acts 1:4–5.
15. See John 20:1–18; 1 Corinthians 15:3–5.
16. See 1 Corinthians 15:6.
17. See Ephesians 1:20.
18. See Ezekiel 28:15.
19. Adapted from *The New Me* Discipleship Curriculum, p. 18.
20. Ibid.
21. See Proverbs 11:2; 16:18; 29:23.
22. "sin," *The New Strong's Complete Dictionary of Bible Words* (Thomas Nelson Publishers, 1996) Greek #264. p. 235.
23. See Matthew 5:21–22,27–28.

24. "condemnation," *Blue Letter Bible* (Strong's Greek #2631, *katakrima,* which means "damnatory sentence, condemnation"; root word *katakrino*). http://cf.blueletterbible.org/lang/lexicon/Lexicon.cfm?Strong's=G2632&version=kjv.

25. "rash," *The Merriam-Webster Dictionary* (Springfield, MA: Merriam-Webster, Inc., 2004), p. 598

Chapter 3: Do Not Be Deceived

1. "sow," *Merriam-Webster Dictionary* (Springfield, MA: Merriam-Webster, Inc., 2004), p. 687.

2. "reap," *The American Heritage® Dictionary of the English Language,* fourth edition (New York: Houghton Mifflin Company, 2004). http://dictionary.reference.com/browse/reap.

3. "consequence," *Dictionary.com Unabridged, v 1.1* (New York: Random House, Inc., 2007). http://dictionary.reference.com/browse/consequence.

4. "guilt," *Merriam-Webster Dictionary,* p. 321.

5. "shame," *The American Heritage® Dictionary of the English Language,* fourth edition (New York: Houghton Mifflin Company, 2004). http://dictionary.reference.com/browse/shame.

6. "saw," *Blue Letter Bible* (Strong's Hebrew #07200, dictionary and word search for *ra'ah*.) http://cf.blueletterbible.org/lang/lexicon/lexicon.cfm?Strongs=H07200&Version=kjv.

7. Ibid. http://cf.blueletterbible.org/lang/lexicon/lexicon.cfm?Strongs=H07200&Version=kjv [Mood-Imperfect See 08811].

8. "anxiety," *Merriam-Webster Dictionary,* p. 32.

9. "depression," *Merriam-Webster Dictionary,* p. 193.

10. "rage," *Merriam-Webster Dictionary*, p. 595.

11. "cud," *Merriam-Webster Dictionary*, p. 170.

12. Catherine C. Harris, "Creature of the Desert, Camel," Tour Egypt web site. http://www.touregypt.net/feature-stories/camel.htm.

13. "Mammals: Camel," San Diego Zoo web site. http://www.sandiegozoo.org/animalbytes/t-camel.html.

14. "flesh," *Merriam-Webster Dictionary*, p. 276.

15. "confess," *Merriam-Webster Dictionary*, p. 151.

16. "repent," *Dictionary.com Unabridged, v 1.1*. http://dictionary.reference.com/browse/repent.

Chapter 4: Forgiven and Set Free

1. "deception," *WordNet® 3.0* (Princeton, NJ: Princeton University, 2007). http://dictionary.reference.com/browse/deception.

2. "misrepresentation," *Dictionary.com Unabridged, v 1.1* (New York: Random House, Inc., 2007). http://dictionary.reference.com/browse/misrepresentation.

3. "honest," *Merriam-Webster Dictionary* (Springfield, MA: Merriam-Webster, Inc., 2004), p. 344.

4. Jon Courson, "Ten Commandments: Do Not Murder—Part 2," lecture on cassette tape (Jacksonville, OR: Applegate Christian Fellowship, 1999).

5. "captive," *Blue Letter Bible*, dictionary and word search for *aichmalōtizō* (Strong's Hebrew #163). http://cf.blueletterbible.org/lang/lexicon/lexicon.cfm?Strongs=G163&Version=kjv.

6. "tangible," *Webster's 21st Century Dictionary* (Nashville, TN: Thomas Nelson Publishers, 1993), p. 1205.

7. "offensive," *Blue Letter Bible*, dictionary and word search for *otseb* (Strong's Hebrew #06090).

http://cf.blueletterbible.org/lang/lexicon/lexicon.
cfm?strongs=H06090&Version=kjv.

Chapter 5: Forgiveness Is Not an Option

1. "bitterness," *Blue Letter Bible*, dictionary and word search for *la`anah* (Strong's Hebrew #3939). http://cf.blueletterbible.org/lang/lexicon/lexicon. cfm?Strongs=H03939&Version=kjv.

2. "bitterness," *Blue Letter Bible*, dictionary and word search for *pikria* (Strong's Greek #4088). http://cf.blueletterbible.org/lang/lexicon/lexicon. cfm?Strongs=G4088&Version=kjv.

3. See Deuteronomy 29:18.

4. "forgive," *Blue Letter Bible*, dictionary and word search for *aphiēmi* (Strong's Greek #863). http:// cf.blueletterbible.org/lang/lexicon/lexicon. cfm?Strongs=G863&Version=kjv.

5. Warren W. Wiersbe, *The Cross of Jesus* (Grand Rapids, MI: Baker Books, 1997), p. 54.

6. The idea for the phrases "forgiveness is and forgiveness is not" was adapted from Sharon Pearce, *Silent Voices Post Abortion Syndrome Healing & Recovery Leader's Manual* (Chula Vista, CA: Silent Voices, 1993), p. 53–55.

7. *The Wesley Bible New King James Version* (Nashville, TN: Thomas Nelson, Inc., 1990), p. 1447.

8. Jay Adams, *From Forgiven to Forgiving* (Amityville, NY: Calvary Press, 1994), p. 12.

9. Ibid., p. 11.

10. Kathleen White, *Corrie ten Boom* (Minneapolis, MN: Bethany House Publishers, 1983), pp. 106–107.

11. "grudge," *Merriam-Webster Dictionary* (Springfield, MA: Merriam-Webster, Inc., 2004), p. 320.

12. "grudge," *Blue Letter Bible* dictionary and word search for *natar* (Strong's Hebrew #05201). http:// cf.blueletterbible.org/lang/lexicon/lexicon.cfm? Strong's=H05201 & T=kjv.

13. Lewis B. Smedes, *Forgive and Forget* (New York, NY: Pocket Books, 1984), p. 57.

14. "tolerate," *WordNet® 3.0* (Princeton, NJ: Princeton University, 2007). http://dictionary.reference.com/browse/tolerate.

15. Adams, p. 57.

16. See Isaiah 43:25; Jeremiah 31:34.

17. Adams, p. 12.

18. Wiersbe, p. 53.

Chapter 6: Set Apart

1. Warren W. Wiersbe, *Be Rich* (Colorado Springs, CO: Chariot Victor Publishing, 1998), pp. 13–14.

2. Ibid., p. 10.

3. "sanctified," *Webster's Ninth New Collegiate Dictionary* (Springfield, MA: Merriam-Webster, 1988), p. 1040.

4. "Historic Royal Speeches and Writings Victoria (r. 1837–1901)," The British Monarchy web site, November 11 2007. http://www.royal.gov.uk/files/pdf/victoria.pdf.

5. Kay Smith, "Dwelling in the Holy of Holies," (Santa Ana, CA: The Word for Today, 2003), lecture on CD.

6. Stephen F. Olford, *The Tabernacle Camping with God* (Grand Rapids, MI: Kregel Publications, 2004), p. 76.

7. John W. Schmitt and J. Carl Laney, *Messiah's Coming Temple Ezekiel's Prophetic Vision of the Future Temple* (Grand Rapids, MI: Kregel Publications, 1997), p. 28.

8. Ibid., p. 28.

9. Ibid., p. 29.

10. Ibid., p. 30.

11. Ibid., p. 30.

12. "contentment," *WordNet® 3.0* (Princeton, NJ: Princeton University, 2007). http://dictionary.reference.com/browse/contentment.

13 Smith, "Dwelling in the Holy of Holies."

14. Elisabeth Elliot, *Passion and Purity* (Grand Rapids, MI: Fleming H. Revell, 1984), p. 21.

15. Charles Spurgeon, "The Rent Veil," sermon delivered at the Metropolitan Tabernacle Pulpit, March 25, 1888. http://www.blueletterbible.org/Comm/charles_spurgeon/sermons/2015.html.

16. Schmitt and Laney, p. 31.

17. *Anna and the King* (New York: 20th Century Fox, 1999).

Chapter 7: Walk Worthy

1. Warren W. Wiersbe, *Be Rich* (Colorado Springs, CO: Chariot Victor Publishing, 1998), pp. 13–14.

2. "faith," *Dictionary.com Unabridged, v 1.1* (New York: Random House, Inc., 2007). http://dictionary.reference.com/browse/faith.

3. Lance Wubbels, ed., *Charles Spurgeon on Prayer A 30-day Devotional Treasury,* (Lynnwood, WA: Emerald Books, 1998), Day 6.

4. *Windtalkers,* Metro-Goldwyn-Mayer Pictures Inc., 2002.

5. Ibid.

6. Ibid.

7. See Joshua 5:14–15.

Chapter 8: A Hope and a Future

1. See Genesis 2:25.

2. "covenant," *Merriam-Webster Dictionary* (Springfield, MA: Merriam-Webster, Inc., 2004), p. 167.

3. Chuck Smith, "Ezekiel 16–20," C2000 Series, *The Word for Today*, August 7, 2005. http://www.blueletterbible.org/Comm/chuck_smith_c2000/Eze/Eze016.html.

4. "debauchery," *Dictionary.com Unabridged, v 1.1* (New York: Random House, Inc., 2007) http://dictionary.reference.com/browse/debauchery.

5. "seduction," *WordNet® 3.0* (Princeton, NJ: Princeton University, 2007). http://dictionary.reference.com/browse/seduction.

6. "yoked," *Dictionary.com Unabridged, v 1.1.* http://dictionary.reference.com/browse/yoked.

7. "unequally," *Dictionary.com Unabridged, v 1.1.* http://dictionary.reference.com/browse/unequally.

Chapter 9: You Are Chosen

1. "called," *The American Heritage® Dictionary of the English Language, Fourth Edition* (New York: Houghton Mifflin Company, 2004). http://dictionary.reference.com/browse/called.

2. "called," *The American Heritage® Dictionary of the English Language, Fourth Edition.* Dictionary.com http://dictionary.reference.com/browse/called.

3. "neighbor," *Merriam-Webster Dictionary* (Springfield, MA: Merriam-Webster, Inc., 2004), p. 484.

4. "paradox," *Collins Essential English Dictionary*, second edition (New York: HarperCollins Publishers, 2006).

5. "paradox," *Merriam-Webster Dictionary*, p. 522.

6. See 2 Corinthians 12:10.

7. See James 2:5.

8. See Matthew 19:30; 20:16; Mark 10:31; Luke 13:30.

9. Matthew 16:24–26; Mark 8:34; Luke 9:23–24; 2 Corinthians 5:14–15.
10. See Acts 20:35.
11. Brian Bell, "Calvary Chapel Murrieta Values—Character" (third in a series), lecture on MP3 (Murrieta, CA: Calvary Chapel Murrieta), January 27, 2008.
12. "calling," *Dictionary of Biblical Imagery* (Downers Grove, IL: InterVarsity Press 1998), p. 133.
13. See Exodus 3:10 (also see Exodus 3–4).
14. See Jeremiah 1:4–10.
15. See Galatians 1:11–24.

Appendix 1: Cruddy Consequences

1. Marshall and Mary Asher, *The Christian's Guide to Psychological Terms* (Bemidji, MN: Focus Publishing, 2004), section 10.
2. Ibid.
3. Ibid.
4. Ibid.
5. Ibid., section 31.

Appendix 3: Profile of an Abuser

1. Adapted from "What Is Domestic Abuse," Tearmann Domestic Violence Services, www.tearmann.net/defndv.htm; "The Abuser," The Broken Spirits Network, www.brokenspirits.com/information/the_abuser.asp. For additional resources, see Patricia Riddle Gaddis, *Dangerous Dating* (Colorado Springs, CO: Waterbrook Press, 2000), pp. 117–119.
2. "Profile of a Batterer," The Sheepfold, June 24, 2008. http://www.thesheepfold.org/victim/victim-batterer.htm.

ABOUT THE AUTHOR

In 1988, Cherie rededicated her life to the Lord, and soon after, God began performing His gentle surgery deep within her heart to heal her of her deep heart hurts. After leading her through a process of recovery, God began impressing on her that she needed to help others with similar hurts and show them how to apply His Word to their lives. In 1993, she co-founded Strong-ARM (Abortion Recovery Ministry) to help women deal with issues of abortion and began teaching purity seminars to help teens make wiser choices. When many women began to attend her workshops for issues other than abortion, she changed the name to The Truth Ministry to better encompass the scope of the work.

In 1999, Cherie wrote her first book titled *Go in Peace!* to help women deal with post-abortion issues. When she was unable to find a curriculum for her workshop that was 100 percent biblically-based, she began writing the *Go in Peace Leader's Manual* and *Go in Peace Student Workbook*. This curriculum was written for individuals attending her seminars who were suffering from any deep heart hurt issues—such as rejection, rape, abortion, and abuse, to name just a few.

In 2001, Cherie and her husband, Keith, opened the non-profit Truth and Hope Foundation in Sofia, Bulgaria, to help women and teens heal from their deep heart hurts. In 2006, she joined the staff of Calvary Chapel Murrieta, where she is the overseer and trainer of the women's counseling ministry. Today, in addition to writing, Cherie loves to travel and teach God's Word and can often be found teaching various topics at women's retreats and teen's seminars. Cherie has two daughters, who are both married to godly young men.

The sale of this book helps to further Cherie and her family's ministry work in the United States, Eastern Europe, and wherever else God sends them.

For more information about Cherie's books,
products or teaching schedule, visit

www.sunflowerpress.net

For more information about the Truth and Hope
Foundation in Sofia, Bulgaria, visit

www.truthandhope.net

To order additional copies of this title call:
1-877-421-READ (7323)
or please visit our Web site at
www.winepressbooks.com

If you enjoyed this quality custom-published book,
drop by our Web site for more books and information.

www.winepressgroup.com
"Your partner in custom publishing."